106 Nguyen-hué
Saigon, Vietnam

I enclose the final chapters, which were delayed by some unpleasant days and nights we have come to expect in Saigon. Vietcong rockets have been exploding within full view of my window in downtown—with a terrifying thunderclap noise, I must admit. The guerrilla gunners are becoming more daring all the time.

One of my worries during the shelling was the manuscript. I took it under my bed for safety. It would have been ironical to see the manuscript of the *Age of the Guerrilla* destroyed by guerrillas.

Sincerely yours,
(signed)
François Sully

AGE OF THE GUERRILLA
The New Warfare

By FRANÇOIS SULLY

Parents' Magazine Press · New York

Background Books are concerned with the broad spectrum of people, places and events affecting the national and international scene. Written simply and clearly, they will engage the minds and interests of people living in a world of great change.

Jacket by Art Klevenz

To my friend Bernard Fall,
1926—Vietnam, 1968

CONTENTS

AUTHOR'S NOTE

Looking into the future is always difficult. But to predict that the decades ahead will probably be remembered as the Age of Guerrilla War is about the safest prophecy that one can make. We are living in an age of change. The world's population is increasing rapidly, and the birth of new nations keeps changing the world's political complexion.

This political fragmentation of the world greatly increases the risk of undeclared wars. Some of the young nations, dissatisfied with their present borders, which, more often than not, were arbitrarily established by their former colonial overlords, undoubtedly will seek to challenge their neighbors to correct what they regard as injustice. Peoples of different religions and mores who, willy-nilly, have been lumped together to form nations will seek to achieve autonomy. And since none of these new nations has the wherewithal for full-scale modern warfare, limited conflicts will seem to them the cheapest way to apply pressure on neighbors, provided the wealthy nations do not supply them with sophisticated weapons.

Old nations proud of their glorious past, such as Portugal, will seek to perpetuate their hegemony over dissenting subjects. Once-great superpowers made arrogant by their own strength will try to maintain their influence over restive satellites. Great Britain's withdrawal from her traditional areas of interest east of Suez will probably trigger a chain of guerrilla wars among former British protectorates, as it also may attract new forms of imperialism.

The hasty departure of the former colonial powers from vast areas of Africa and Asia has left an emotional vacuum, because in many cases the colonial ruler had successfully undermined the existing indigenous culture. The leaders of newly born nations are now attempting to fill this vacuum with new and old dreams. Once the initial dream of freedom has been fulfilled, the new dreams are either centered on economic development or focused on the past. Indonesia's Sukarno belonged to the generation of post-decolonization dreamers. To him, reviving the territorial ambitions of the 14th-century Madjapahit empire justified a permanent state of war against neighboring Malaya.

A similar dream has since been revived by the Filipino guerrillas who are burning to invade Sabah (North Borneo) in the name of the long-forgotten Sultan of Sulu. Meantime, a small guerrilla war is being waged between Thailand and Cambodia around the ancient temple of Preah Vihear, remnant of a defunct Asian kingdom that both claim as theirs. Historic antipathies and prejudices are deeply rooted among the new nations. And, of course, there is Mao Tsetung, the Chinese visionary who has dreams of People's War in at least twelve Latin-American countries—though he sharply disagrees with Latin revolutionaries on how to wage it: whether guns or politics should be in command.

CHAPTER 1

A VERY PERSONAL VIEW OF GUERRILLA WAR

If I have learned anything in twenty years of watching guerrillas in action, it is that war can become a way of life. In more fortunate lands, peace represents stability and the familiar, whereas war portends chaos and the unknown. But for millions of Burmese, Laotians, and Vietnamese, the tables have been turned: it is the prospect of peace that is unsettling. Civil war, in effect, has become the status quo. Americans—whose own lives are increasingly disturbed by this faraway fighting—naturally tend to exaggerate the degree of disturbance to the people on the spot. They have never watched the amazing detachment of the Vietnamese farmer, plowing his meager rice paddy as bombs burst nearby. I remember as a young soldier firing angry salvos of artillery fire directly over the heads of peasants stoically harvesting their crop. Safe in my bunker, I was nonetheless considerably more rattled than the stooping rice farmers out in the open, going methodically about their work.

11

When at last I was discharged from the army, I became a farmer myself and began to operate a 200-acre tea plantation in the Central Highland jungles about half a day's drive from Saigon. I soon discovered, like the peasants around me, that the guerrillas who were even then roaming the countryside were the least of our worries. Tigers and panthers were far more menacing, and the worst aggressor of all was the tropical rain forest whose invasions we were constantly combating. To find workers for my land, I had to trek eight days into the mountains and bargain with the isolated Montagnard tribes. With supreme assurance, they would guide me around the guerrilla forces lurking about in the hope of ambushing government patrols. Once, showing even greater confidence, they sent me a contingent of bare-chested young girls to harvest my crop of tea.

The Vietnamese, I discovered soon after my arrival in Vietnam, have even managed to fit the war into their elaborately superstitious outlook on life. My first brush with the omnipresent Vietnamese spirit world came when my plantation caretaker suddenly died for no apparent reason. To the local residents, there was no question about who was responsible: a powerful genie who, it was said, lived in a large banyan tree on the estate. In our haste to clear cultivable land we had damaged the tree, and now, I was told, the genie was exacting his revenge. All my laborers promptly quit, and I had to abandon the place. Years later, Catholic refugees occupied the same land and, after taking the precaution of exorcising the genie, cleared away all the trees. In no time at all—perhaps by coincidence, perhaps not—the guerrillas moved in. Violent death returned to the area, and the peasants were sure they knew why.

Occultism, however, is by no means confined to the peasantry. One of my closest Vietnamese friends, General Pham

Van Dong, would never start a military operation on Wandering Souls' Day, the day on which Vietnamese honor their parents' graves. Former Premier Nguyen Khanh was careful to consult an astrologer before launching the coup that put him in power, and his famous goatee was grown on his soothsayer's advice.

Even the staunchly Catholic Diems were not exempt from superstition. Madame Nhu had an Indian astrologer attached to her retinue, and her brother-in-law, President Ngo Dinh Diem, once sent secret emissaries to North Vietnam to seek out the remains of his elder brother, who had been killed by the Communists. Without proper burial, Diem believed, his brother's ghost was sure to return to haunt the living. This near-universal belief explains why the Vietcong will go to such perilous lengths to retrieve and bury their dead. Sometimes, individual guerrillas supervise the digging of their own grave even before the battle, because, as one put it to me, "I know my fate is to die."

All Vietnamese, in fact, whether Christian or Buddhist or Communist, like to have some supernatural protector—a religion, a cult, a genie—to shield them from evil spirits. For the Vietcong, to a great extent, membership in the Communist Party plays that role, which may help to explain why the rank and file of guerrillas proudly call themselves True Believers.

There is one sort of protector, however, that no Vietnamese really wants, and that is a foreign one. Vietnam needed no Mao Tse-tung or Vo Nguyen Giap to elucidate the phenomenon of a people's war, in which an entire population is mobilized to resist outsiders. The country had been through it all before, beginning in 1283 when powerful Mongol armies began driving toward her borders. Should the tiny kingdom try to resist so overwhelming an on-

slaught? The Emperor gathered the elders of his realm at
Dien Hong and put the question to them. His subjects
promptly vowed to defend their country to the death. "And
if our soldiers are killed," the elders promised, "we, the old
men, will carry on the fight, with the help of the women
and children." The records of the Dien Hong Congress are
among Vietnam's most cherished documents. A young
North Vietnamese once told me that if Lyndon B. Johnson
had only read them, he would have understood why Hanoi
kept up the fight against such formidable odds.

My whole experience in Vietnam convinces me that intervention by foreigners—however well-meaning—can only
prolong the country's twenty-year-old civil war and make
it fiercer. For the tragedy of French—American involvement
in Vietnam is that they have created an unintended but
nonetheless difficult dilemma for the Vietnamese people.
The intelligent, patriotic Vietnamese is currently torn between two equally fervent aspirations: liberation of his country from foreign influence, and personal freedom from political oppression and economic distress. As most Vietnamese
see it, Hanoi offers only the hope of freedom from foreign
influence while Saigon offers only the hope of personal freedom, and thus is born a terrible tension for the citizen who
deeply yearns for both. Each side can hold out only the hope
of half-fulfillment, and this is the main reason why the
country is still divided.

The dilemma, of course, is by no means entirely of foreign manufacture. Ho Chi Minh made a disastrous tactical
error when he hitched his nationalist wagon to a Communist star and thus gave France the opportunity to split the
Vietnamese independence movement along ideological
lines. Had Ho fought only in the name of liberation and
socialism, his cause would doubtless have prevailed completely, and Vietnam would have been spared her protracted

agony. Ho's links to world Communism turned an anti-colonial war into a civil war and then into an international one.

But whoever is responsible for the deep psychological dilemma of the Vietnamese, its effects are readily apparent every day, particularly in the delicate relationship between the South Vietnamese and their American allies. The Vietnamese are probably the brightest people in all Southeast Asia, yet to American officers assigned to Vietnamese units, they often seem maddeningly slow, dull, and inefficient. As a Vietnamese colonel once explained to me: "We think that any Vietnamese officer who needs a foreign adviser must be a pretty bad officer. Our cousins on the Vietcong side seem to get along without any *co van* (advisers). So when the Americans are around, many Vietnamese act stupid. In fact, they are dragging their feet or playing dumb because they are too polite to tell their *co van* to mind his own business. The ineffectiveness of Vietnamese officers simply reflects the inner reservations of many of us about the objectives and methods of this war. Our top generals who tell you that they want to fight to the end are lying."

And from the Vietnamese who have managed to opt out of the war come variations on the same theme. A deserter from the army, one of tens of thousands hiding in Saigon, recently told me: "If this war were for national survival against the Chinese or Cambodians, I would fight willingly. But frankly, most of us are tired of fighting other Vietnamese while our leaders enjoy the good life in Saigon. If we lose this war, I will lose what? My Honda motorbike and perhaps the American condensed milk for my morning coffee. Do you think these things are worth getting killed for?"

The suave son of a wealthy Saigon lawyer whom I encountered on a university campus in California had a similar attitude. "Yes," he confessed, "I am here to evade the draft in my country. Sure, I know that if the other side wins my family will lose a lot. Perhaps we'll have to go into exile for a while. But you should understand that the price in lives, destruction, and hardship that we will have to pay merely to prevent Ho Chi Minh from visiting Saigon is far too high. We may dislike Ho and his drab bunch of followers, but we must admit that they are Vietnamese like ourselves. Furthermore, Communist or not, they will need educated people—perhaps me—to run and rebuild the country. Never forget that, still today, it's the same 200 families that provide the leadership in both the South and the North."

Years of foreign influence have done the Vietnamese very little good and a great deal of harm. For one thing, a deep wedge has been driven between city and countryside, cutting off any real communication or sympathy between the Western-educated urban intelligentsia and the tranquil, self-contained Vietnamese peasantry. American training and Western-cut uniforms have transformed Vietnamese officers into foreigners in their own land, and the sight of U.S. technological wonders vastly reinforces the contempt these officers feel for the simple life of the farmer. In effect, the Western presence in Vietnam has helped to create a denatured class of Vietnamese who look toward Washington, Paris, or Rome, rather than among their own people, for inspiration and strength. To me, there is no sight more pathetic than the perfumed, bejeweled, high-heeled ladies of Saigon society paying a perfunctory, condescending visit to some rural hamlet as part of a government-sponsored charity program.

In many ways, in fact, the generals who rule in Saigon

today are even more remote from their countrymen than
Ngo Dinh Diem ever was. And unfortunately, it is through
the eyes of this small Westernized minority that we West-
erners get our own misguided perception of Vietnam's
problems. Thus, although some of the members of this
minority may busy themselves with an effort to establish
the institutions of Western liberal democracy, such debates
are largely irrelevant and meaningless to all but perhaps
100,000 of the country's 15,000,000 citizens. The ability and
integrity of the local *Dai Uy,* the army district commander,
is of far more pressing interest to the ordinary Vietnamese
than the question of whether to establish a bicameral legislature.

In fact, most Vietnamese want and expect their government to be essentially paternalistic. Its function is to rule
wisely, to appoint honest officials, to provide justice, and to
let the peasant villages select their own Councils of Elders
to run purely local matters. The farmers see neither sense
nor attraction in the prospect of electing civilian politicians to represent them in Saigon. I am afraid that even if
the present military junta should submit to a liberal constitution, Western democracy—as we have experienced it—will
be totally unworkable in Vietnam.

In more ways than one, Vietnam's problems are found in
other parts of Asia, as they are also in Latin America and in
Africa. Here, too, political insurgencies threaten the stability of unstable new governments. And more often than
not, bullets and bombs are used as substitutes for political
solutions. Not everywhere, of course, but in many cases, in-
corruptible administrators and efficient officials would defeat the guerrillas more effectively. This, in any case, is my
very personal view of the problem.

NEEDED:
AN UNDERSTANDING
OF GUERRILLA WARS

Examination of contemporary insurgencies reveals the fact
that, contrary to a widespread assumption, neither poverty,
economic hardship, nor even orders from a central worldwide political conspiracy are the main causes of these wars.

Most frequently people adjust to hardships, accept their
fate with resignation, or remain apathetic like the dirt-poor
Indians of South America. It then takes a dedicated leader
such as the Argentine Che Guevara to arouse them—with
great difficulty. Periodically, it is true, hunger leads the
homeless poor of Calcutta to riot; but it is the less destitute
Mizos in the forests of Assam who have taken up arms
against the New Delhi government. Poverty pockets may
breed crime, violence, and other social ills, but they rarely
explode into sustained guerrilla wars.

One striking demonstration of this thesis is that even relatively well-off South Vietnamese farmers, and some workers
as well, are sympathetic to Vietcong guerrillas, while their
much less affluent brethren in North Vietnam support Ho
Chi Minh's "liberation war" against the pro-West Saigon
government. Economics, then, cannot explain the Vietnam
war. True, economic factors—and especially underdevelop-
ment—often play a role in guerrilla wars, but they are not
dominant. Widespread political awareness and social consciousness among a people, coupled with a sentiment of
revolt toward a regime that has failed to make itself popular, often are prevailing factors in guerrilla wars.

Equally important, in fact, is the geography of the land:
A guerrilla movement needs room to expand and sanctu-
aries out of reach of its enemies in which to regroup,

recuperate, and train. But even the most favorable geographical assets are not enough to bring certain success. Che Guevara after six months gave up his attempt to stir up guerrilla warfare in the former Belgian Congo because, as he put it later: "The human material was not adequate. The leaders were corrupt, and they quarreled."

What, then, are the necessary ingredients to launch a guerrilla war and lead it to success? Some analysts think that the existence of a quasi-religious belief among a small group of political activists, and the presence of a charismatic leader are indispensable conditions. Activists must have a cause appealing to a larger number of men forming either a racial entity or a social or religious grouping. Guerrillas without a cause shared by a growing segment of their society (10 percent to 20 percent of popular support is enough at the beginning) remain outlaws.

There are exceptions. But guerrillas rarely fight for the immediate economic and social improvement of their lot, even if economic betterment is one of their objectives.

In most guerrilla wars the fight is often crystallized around one purely emotional issue: self-determination, racial equality, independence, or, as in Cyprus, *enosis* (reunion with a motherland). Frequently, this issue has a romantic appeal for one segment of the population. In Cuba, for example, the political revolution preached by Fidel Castro initially struck a responsive chord not among the poor and dispossessed, but among intellectuals and businessmen of the bourgeoisie. When the character of the Cuban revolution then changed from a political protest movement into a social revolution, many intellectuals and bourgeoisie went into exile.

Another preconceived idea, especially in the West, is the suspicion that all guerrilla movements are either Communist-led or Communist-dominated. Nothing, in fact, could be further from reality. A still incomplete survey of all guerrilla movements taking place throughout the world since the end of World War II reveals that movements espousing either a socialist or nationalist cause outnumbered Communist-directed insurgencies by at least two to one.

Most of the guerrilla movements in the Middle East and in Africa have been motivated by Arab or African nationalism. Communism played a minor role in these movements, although aid from Communist-bloc countries was often offered and accepted. It is true, however, that the Communist system of cell organization has been used by many guerrilla movements to protect their undercover apparatus.

But even the fact that a guerrilla movement is Communist-led does not mean that Marxist motives are either its sole source of inspiration or its main cause. During the war in Indochina, it was traditional Vietnamese nationalism, a thirst for independence, that provided the ideological assets of the Vietminh movement. The causes of the Vietminh insurgency were related far more to this genuine desire for independence and to the peasants' "hunger for land" than to the fact that Ho Chi Minh was the founder of the Indochinese Communist Party. As General Hoang Van Thai, former Chief of Staff of the Vietminh army at Dienbienphu, said in explaining the motivation of his guerrillas, "We were possessed by an invincible force, which the enemy lacked: It was, in the heart of man, love for his motherland, the refusal to live in slavery." And General Thai used these words to describe the emotional content of the Vietminh war: "We were faced with this dilemma: either crawling under bombs to win back dignity for our people, or a cowardly renunciation of the fight and desertion to save one's life." Thus, to say that Dienbienphu was a Communist victory is to give the Marxist-Leninists undue credit. It was mainly the patriotism of Vietnamese peasant-guerrillas that finally prevailed.

Though, of course, differences do exist between the Indochinese war of the 1950's and the 1960's war in Vietnam, it would be a mistake to maintain that nationalism no longer plays a role in the Vietcong movement. The main appeal of the Liberation Front to the Vietnamese peasantry lies in slogans such as this: "Vietnam is one, the Vietnamese people are one. The plot of perpetually partitioning Vietnam is in flagrant contradiction with her natural conditions, historical realities, and the sacred rights of her people; therefore it is checked by the iron will for struggle of both the North and South zones."

Obviously, not all Vietnamese agree with this exalted version of the Front's objective; but to ignore the significance of nationalism is a serious mistake, perhaps one cause for the fact that it became so protracted.

The lesson of all this is that no government, however well-meaning, can prevent a small group of dedicated men from starting a guerrilla war in some remote or favorable area (city slums, for example). But success or failure in defeating guerrillas lies largely in the authorities' approach to the problem. Mere repressive measures generally are not sufficient to eradicate the roots of an insurgency, which may be revived once law-enforcement agencies start lowering their guard. Most lasting results can be obtained if the government concerned analyzes the intertwined political, sociological, and economic grievances forming the cause— either apparent or hidden—of the insurgency.

Two pertinent questions may be asked: "Will brushfire wars continue to flare up with increasing frequency in the world's less stable areas?" and, "What will be the role of limited wars in the future?" The answer to the first question, unfortunately, seems to be, Yes: Guerrilla wars have become part of the international equation of power, as they have become an accepted form of protest.

Regarding the second question, some observers, among them Walter Lippmann, believe that the 20th-century phenomenon of limited (or whatever other names we may call them) wars reflects the political limitations of the superpowers in enforcing a world order. Nor are these great powers any longer able to arbitrate the quarrels of lesser states (Israel and Jordan, for example) and of enforcing their decision.

Occasionally, the great powers seem to believe that they are running the world because such or such guerrilla army is using their weaponry. But guerrillas, usually, are an intractable lot. Both Moscow and Peking, not to mention other countries, are supplying millions of dollars' worth of equipment to North Vietnam, but Hanoi has yet to take sides in the ideological dispute between Russia and China. The same, to a lesser extent, could be said of the South Vietnamese military leaders; despite the $100,000,000,000 the United States has lavished on their country since 1955, the South Vietnamese continue to make a mockery of American recommendations for social and economic reforms.

In the case of Vietnam, the two local participants have become largely unmanageable by Peking, Moscow, or Washington. China and the Soviet Union were no more able to protect North Vietnam against American acts of war than the mighty United States was able to shelter Saigon from the harassing attacks of Ho Chi Minh's supporters. For once, the puppets were leading the show.

What has happened, in effect, is that the superpowers

have been dethroned by the smaller nations. Great Britain is ignored in Nigeria, in Cyprus, and even in tiny Mauritius. Russia is not feared by the Israelis, and Washington cannot impose its will on a fourth-rate power such as Vietnam. "We are now faced with the fact," observes Lippmann, "that there is a radical disconnection between little nations which have emerged since the last World War and the great powers which once ruled them and gave a certain order to the world. . . . The great powers cannot combine to govern the world; the world is not governed."

One major reason for this, of course, is the nuclear stalemate, in which the small nations have found that they can defy the great powers and make war among themselves with relative immunity from serious reprisals by the big ·powers. The pygmy nations fight their wars with passion, and the big powers can do little more than keep them supplied with ammunition, since no one dares to intervene and break up the fight.

Another aspect of the problem is that the superpowers can manipulate guerrilla wars and escalate them into sizable geographically limited conflicts (Korea, Vietnam) and thereby wage indirect war with each other without the risk of reciprocal annihilation that direct confrontation would create.

"Since 1945," wrote Roger Hilsman in his Foreword for *People's War, People's Army,* "there have been about two dozen 'limited' wars, many of them involving guerrilla tactics. General Maxwell Taylor had a special study made of conflicts since 1945 and found that while these have been 'limited' in terms of weapons and geography, they have not been minor. The average length of these conflicts has been two years, and the average number of troops engaged has been 600,000."

A solution to this state of affairs would be for the great powers to pledge nonintervention in the quarrels of smaller nations. This would not entirely eliminate guerrilla wars, but it would at least limit them to an exchange of blows between midgets. And since guerrillas usually need the attention of the outside world to stay in the fight, one side or the other would eventually lose heart or exhaust its resources and desist.

Another solution would be a return to the concept of regional spheres of influence, each superpower being responsible for maintaining law and order among its client states without risking interference from its rivals. This is pretty much what the government of President Charles de Gaulle did seek to do for the fourteen-nation community of French-speaking African states. At the first sign of trouble, say in Gabon or in the Central Africa Republic, de Gaulle dispatches a company or two of paratroopers to quell the turmoil. The outside world has barely time to notice before the trouble is over. Speed, in such cases, is of the essence. There is tacit agreement among the African states that this is the way things should be. To be sure, there is less risk of Chinese or Russian intervention in Chad or Dahomey than, say, in Southeast Asia.

Churchmen of all creeds have traditionally avoided taking sides in partisan political conflicts. The rule no longer holds, however. A small yet growing number of clergymen —Protestant as well as Roman Catholic—see in the papal encyclical *Populorum progressio* a religious precedent for siding with a social revolution. Like the young Guatemalan priest Camillo Torres, these clerics have decided that they will not remain silent while desperate men are taking up arms in hope of creating a better future for themselves and mankind.

Out of sheer desperation, perhaps, to bring social justice to their impoverished missions some missionaries in Brazil and Guatemala have met with guerrilla leaders and adopted a sympathetic attitude toward the cause of rebel violence. These priests feel deeply that guerrilla warfare can be a legitimate reaction against violence instituted by an oppressive regime; that "it is right to rebel for a just cause." To the question, "Can a priest forfeit his responsibilities as a citizen?" the answer, for the priestly rebels, is a challenging negative.

Western missionaries and priests are not the only churchmen to feel that the age of guerrilla warfare as a social protest is dawning. After much meditation, some South Vietnamese Buddhist monks have decided that their religion requires a total involvement in the struggle. Several Buddhist monks have joined the insurgent "Liberation Front for South Vietnam." One, known as Thien Hao, is a member of the Front's central committee. During the February 1968 fighting near Hué, the ancient capital of Central Vietnam, at least one monk, Thich Gia Luyen, was killed "while carrying out a revolutionary mission."

At the same time, the Venerable Thich Don Hau, Buddhist superior in Central Vietnam, left his Thien Mu monastery to live with Vietcong guerrillas in the mountains. From there he went on the radio to encourage the Buddhist faithful to "join with the people and fight side by side with them for the great cause." "Hail Buddha Amida!" chanted Don Hau in conclusion.

Obviously, not all churchmen will emulate Camillo Torres or Thich Gia Luyen. But the fact is that guerrilla warfare for social aims is becoming increasingly an excusable, if not acceptable, way of conduct for clerics who feel that the days of contemplative faith are well past.

COUNTERINSURGENCY

"The counterinsurgent cannot win by imitating the insurgent, because he is alien in the revolutionary situation,
and because his tasks are precisely the opposite of those of
the guerrilla."

Robert Taber in *The War of the Flea*

Counterinsurgency is not guerrilla warfare, and this is not
an artificial distinction; it arises from the practical reality
of fighting the two types of war. For example, it is one thing
to destroy a railroad as a guerrilla insurgent; it is quite another to defend the same railroad against sabotage or attack
by guerrillas.

It may take five well-trained saboteurs two weeks to plan
and execute the destruction of a railroad bridge, whereas
protecting the same bridge may tie up a 39-man platoon of
troops for an indefinite period of time. The protection of a
large bridge may require a full 125-man company with no
other useful mission. For this reason, acquiring and cor-
relating the intelligence that will allow counterinsurgency
forces to defeat the saboteurs before they can carry out their
mission is often the cheapest way to fight guerrillas. A counterguerrilla force, to be efficient, must be well informed and
capable of responding quickly to intelligence.

Counterinsurgency operations, nevertheless, are always
expensive. Generally speaking, the cost of killing a South
Vietnamese guerrilla exceeds $500,000. By comparison, in-
ducing a guerrilla to give himself up requires an investment
of only $500 in psychological operations. In roadless regions,
an investment of $1,000,000 or $2,000,000 per square mile in
lines of communications may effectively prevent the development of an insurgent base and eventually provide

economic benefits that will offset the cost of the initial investment.

There is no such thing as a fixed ratio of troops needed to defeat an insurgency. The oft-quoted figure of ten policemen or soldiers to catch a guerrilla is totally arbitrary, although it may be used as a rule of thumb for specific guerrilla fire-fights. In Malaysia, British and Commonwealth forces achieved victory with a ratio of 10 to 1. But in Cyprus the British failed with a ratio of 50 to 1 in their favor, and the French were unable to "pacify" Algeria despite a favorable ratio of 100 to 1. In the early days of the Vietnam conflict, 300,000 South Vietnamese police and military forces did not quash the embryonic Vietcong insurgency triggered by some 3,500 poorly equipped guerrillas without appreciable outside support.

Many things, in fact, depend on how successful the insurgents are in recruiting and motivating an ever-expanding number of followers. To quote Robert Taber in *The War of the Flea,* "Without the consent and active aid of the people, the guerrilla would be merely a bandit, and could not long survive. If, on the other hand, the counterinsurgent could claim this same support, the guerrillas would not exist."

Guerrilla warfare has been practiced successfully many times in history. There have been, however, few successful counterinsurgency operations.

URBAN GUERRILLA WARFARE

One of the loudest controversies among students of limited warfare is whether urban guerrilla warfare is feasible. Urban warfare is generally rejected by Mainland Chinese military strategists, who had disastrous experiences with it during their civil war against the Kuomintang. In their view, cities can be deadly traps for guerrillas; with no place to retreat, they become easy prey for police repression.

City dwellers, the Chinese argue, are not the best guerrilla material; they may fight for a while but then become discouraged and give up the cause for some immediate economic advantage. Furthermore, it is difficult for city guerrillas to escape encirclement by the enemy. At the most, cities should be used as logistical bases and sources of financial revenue. They also offer good possibilities for recruiting the skilled personnel that a guerrilla movement needs to operate its war industries in the countryside. In other words, cities should be used as a source for men and material to be used elsewhere.

Urban resistance movements, if they can be organized, often try to carry on their activities under a legal cover, such as a labor union or a religious movement, and usually confine themselves to protest marches and strikes designed to disorganize the administrative machinery of the state. Labor unions, lay religious organizations, and student movements offer opportunities for political penetration— although the risks of being detected and caught are great in the long range. The threat of urban disorders can force a government to tie up many troops that otherwise would be available to fight guerrillas in the countryside.

Problems of command also arise. Castro felt that the urban branch of a guerrilla movement should always be subordinate to a rural headquarters and confine itself to the mission entrusted to it. Che Guevara thought urban guerrilla bands should remain small "and should not emerge into the open until the insurgents besiege the city" because "the risks and consequence of exposure are tremendous."

"It is fundamental to recognize," Che Guevara wrote, "that a suburban guerrilla band can never spring up of its own accord . . . the suburban guerrilla will always be under the direct orders of chiefs located in another [rural] zone. The function of urban guerrilla bands will not be to carry independent actions but to coordinate its activities with overall strategic plans."

In South Vietnam, the command post for urban guerrilla organizations operating in Saigon (perhaps 4,000 to 5,000 men) is located in a rural area 30 to 40 miles north of the city, but close enough for rapid liaison. Cell leaders of urban organizations are trained at this rural command post, where they acquire a proletarian mentality. The highest-ranking guerrilla leader for Saigon, the architect Huynh Tan Phat, communicates with his urban cells and rural units through a complex network of couriers, many of them women.

There is always the risk that the urban wing of the movement will lose contact with the realities of the struggle in the countryside. To avoid this, the South Vietnamese Liberation Front included Saigon in a greater metropolitan area with a population of 3,000,000 to 4,000,000, thus enforcing the political leadership of the countryside over the city.

The 1968 Tet Offensive of the Vietcong against thirty Vietnamese cities wrote a new chapter in the history of urban guerrilla warfare. At 3 A.M. on January 31, Hué, the ancient capital of Vietnam, was noiselessly infiltrated by some 4,000 sandal-shod guerrillas. Well disciplined, they entered without being detected by either the police or the military garrison. Hué (population, 140,000) is the headquarters for the 1st Vietnamese Infantry Division and an important provincial capital.

The guerrillas, who had come down from the nearby

Nam Hoa Mts., were armed with rapid-firing Chinese AK-47 submachine guns and B-40 antitank rockets, both superb weapons for street fighting. They found ready assistance from local guides, and in less than two hours all United States (a 300-man advisory detachment) and Vietnamese forces were neutralized and most administrative buildings occupied. The attackers did not try to launch frontal assaults against isolated pockets of Vietnamese and U.S. soldiers who resisted with determination, but they controlled the rest of the town and managed to free 1,300 political prisoners from the city jail.

Within Hué, the guerrillas captured and summarily executed some 900 government officials. Perhaps 200 more were taken prisoner in the mountains. Typically, very little resistance was offered by the 1,200 black-uniformed Revolutionary Development cadre men working in teams of 50 in the suburban villages.

It took twenty-five days for a regiment of U.S. and Vietnamese Marines, supported by heavy tanks, artillery, and aircraft, to recapture Hué house by house. In the process, the city suffered damage estimated at $20,000,000 and perhaps 5,000 civilian casualties. The hard-core guerrilla units —organized in 16 battalions—had already left the town when the Marines recaptured the old Citadel, which was defended by a screen of local guerrillas who fought to the bitter end. Some 1,800 citizens were later arrested for collaboration with the guerrilla organization.

Hué demonstrated that with good weapons, good tactics, and support from the citizenry guerrillas can resist against a force equipped with modern armament. In daylight, the guerrillas remained hidden in houses, where they obtained food from fearful civilians. They moved only after dark to carry out raids against U.S. lines. American officers later claimed that 4,000 of the 8,000 guerrillas who had entered Hué were eventually killed, either in the ground fighting or as a result of B-52 bombing raids on suspected Vietcong headquarters on the outskirts of the city. The Marines alone accounted for 2,300 enemy killed within the city. Marine battalions engaged in street fighting suffered 50 percent casualties, dead and wounded. As one Marine colonel later explained, "We had to destroy the city in order to save it."

THE GREEK CIVIL WAR

Roughly the size of the State of Alabama, with a population of nearly 10,000,000, Greece is essentially a maritime country notable for its long, indented coastline dotted with numerous inlets and deep gulfs. Over the centuries Greece has been a land of invasion open to varied influences from the Mediterranean area, the Middle East and the troublesome part of Eastern Europe known as the Balkans. Her mainland neighbors are Albania on the west, Yugoslavia and Bulgaria on the north, while Turkey just touches her on the east. Three of these neighbors are under Communist regimes, a fact providing part of the background to the clash of ideologies still taking place among Greek society.

Terrain, always an influencing factor in any type of military operations, is in Greece ideally suited for guerrilla warfare. The craggy mountains of Greece cover more than two-thirds of the mainland and are the homes of about 40 percent of the population. The land can only support poor and widely separated villages. Mountain dwellers eke out a bare existence. The remainder of the population is concentrated in cities with about one-fifth of all Greeks living in the crowded Athens-Piraneus area. There are no large cities in the lofty mountains where poor soils can only feed herds of sheep and goats. In the narrow plains, tobacco, grapes, olives and dried fruits are cultivated for export. Lack of fuel and scarcity of raw material have retarded industrial development.

Under the Axis occupation of Greece during World War II, the Greek Communist Party (KKE) formed and directed a resistance army (ELAS), which spent more effort in trying to eliminate rival guerrilla bands in the mountains than in harassing the occupiers. After liberation in 1944, ELAS, then 55,000 strong, attempted to crush the Greek National Army (GNA) but was defeated after speedy British military intervention. In spite of subsequent agreements, however, the Communist organization remained.

In 1946 a new insurgent force called the Democratic Army came into being in the hills of Greece, with assistance from across the borders of Communist Albania, Yugoslavia, and Bulgaria. Employing the methods of guerrilla warfare, the Democratic Army made considerable headway against the poorly equipped Greek army and police forces.

In 1947 President Truman decided to send military assistance to Greece, taking over from the British the burden of bolstering the weak and embattled Athens government. This move halted the guerrillas' progress.

After a year of stalemate, during which the National Army was re-equipped and retrained, the Communists resumed their attacks on a larger scale. General Markos Vafiades, the ELAS chief political commissar during the Germano-Italian occupation, was made commander of the Communist army. A onetime tobacco farmer who had served in the Greek cavalry, General Markos had the look of a stout Greek peasant. A fairly popular leader, Markos was able to recruit some 23,000 armed guerrillas, of whom 20 percent were women, with about 8,000 replacements in training centers in Eastern Europe. General Markos kept his troops in small, semi-independent units and concentrated upon raids and sabotage against government installations. Enemies of the guerrillas were terrorized by the pervasive fear of reprisals; few Greek villages were immune from the threat of surprise night raids. Wisely, guerrilla units gave way before advances of the GNA and then filtered back when the way was clear again. In this way, Markos' forces could hold their own, keep their personnel losses to a minimum, and give up very little territory.

A sound intelligence network is vital to guerrilla operations of any size. In this area, Markos' guerrillas were magnificently aided by "self-defense" units and informers in most of the populated centers. These secret guerrilla cells operated clandestinely through the YIAFKA organization and kept the guerrilla force informed of all movements of the Greek army. In addition to this vital mission of spying, YIAFKA members collected funds, carried supplies, recruited new members, and proselytized actively among Greek army personnel. They were also used to identify and eliminate persons suspected of informing for the government. By 1947, YIAFKA could rely on 50,000 active members and some 750,000 sympathizers throughout Greece. Thus, it can be said that at least 10 percent of the total population was involved in one way or another in support of the guerrilla movement.

Providing his guerrillas with food, clothes, and weapons presented Markos with a difficult problem. The largest units were established in twenty to thirty main bases in the mountains, and supplying them was hazardous because of terrain, distance, and the risk of interception by Greek police. Markos solved this problem by using trains of pack animals—donkeys and horses—moving mainly at night. Regional support units of fifty to sixty men each were assigned the task of quartermastering for the combat units and of taking care of their sick and wounded. These regional units were forbidden to leave their area of responsibility. Whenever the Greek army launched a clearing operation, they split up and hid until the all-clear signal.

At the beginning of 1948, some 23,000 guerrillas were holding their own in the field against 118,000 government troops supported by two Spitfire squadrons of the Greek Air Force. Despite its overwhelming numerical advantage, the army seemed unable either to seal the northern border or to conduct an effective guerrilla campaign.

Markos' true difficulties began with the 1948 split between Tito of Yugoslavia and Premier Joseph Stalin of the U.S.S.R. He stubbornly refused to take sides in the ideological rift and continued to use both Yugoslav and Bulgarian bases despite the promptings of other Greek Communist leaders, who insisted that he should break totally with Tito.

General Nicholas Zacharias, Greek Communist Party Secretary, who had spent the war in a German concentration camp, charged Markos with "Trotskyite behavior" and expelled him from the party as a "deserter from the democratic movement." Markos was sent to Rumania for treatment of "mental disorders" and imprisonment, and Stalinist Zacharias took over command of the powerful force of Communist guerrillas.

In November 1948 the guerrilla high command reorganized its units along conventional lines with brigades, divisions, and corps. A brigade comprised 600 to 800 men; a division, two or three brigades; and a corps, two or three divisions. Zacharias insisted on meeting the Greek army with full-scale attacks in hope of dealing the final blow leading to seizure of power. The situation had the makings of a limited war on the pattern that was to become familiar in Korea two years later.

But after Tito's denial of supply routes into northern Greece, many things went wrong for the Communist army. The KKE leadership was reported divided. One faction, favoring international Communism as prescribed by Moscow, put its trust in Stalin. The other favored a form of national Communism and collaboration with Tito. In the confusion, the Greek army with expert military guidance by U.S. General James Van Fleet regained the initiative.

Under Van Fleet's insistence, energetic measures were taken against the Communist movement. One of the most effective was the systematic removal of the population from insecure areas. Eventually, 700,000 uprooted peasants lived in towns controlled by the government. This radical measure deprived the guerrillas of the steady stream of intelligence and supplies that had flowed through the YIAFKA organization. They now had to fight in relative isolation in 36 separate mountain ranges, under constant harassment by 51 U.S.-supplied Helldiver fighter-bombers.

Van Fleet also increased the Greek army to 160,000 men, who were sent in the dead of winter to comb the mountains, turning the guerrillas into hunted refugees. Later, Albania ceased aiding the Democratic Army, thus forcing it to move the bulk of its troops and stores to Bulgaria—a highly dangerous operation. A large number of guerrillas were killed or captured when the Greek army conducted a series of operations in the Peloponnesus, the large expanse of land at the southern tip of Greece, separated from the mainland by the Gulf of Corinth. Then the army worked its way northward, toward the satellite borders.

In August 1949 the guerrilla high command made a strategic error. It decided to defend two major strongholds in northwestern Greece. The result was the destruction of the bulk of the guerrilla army after two successive government offensives. By the end of the year a few small, starving, and desperate guerrilla bands were left in the frigid mountains, their entire effort directed toward survival.

Lack of self-reliance and of unity among the leadership defeated the guerrilla movement (years later North Vietnam cautiously avoided the same mistakes). On October 16, 1949, the clandestine Democratic Army radio announced that its forces had decided on a cease-fire "to prevent the complete destruction of Greece." In explanation it declared that it had been forced to retreat in the face of material superiority of the U.S.-supported Greek government and of Tito's defection and treason. In fact, the war was over.

Figures released by the Greek government indicate that between June 1945 and March 1949, the Democratic Army losses totaled 70,027, including 27,931 who surrendered. Government casualty figures were given as 10,927 killed, 23,251 wounded, and 3,756 missing. Some 3,200 civilians were executed by the rebels, and 731 were killed by mines or other causes.

CHAPTER 2

THE ARAB WORLD: CROSSROADS AND BATTLE GROUND

The Arab world represents such a vital crossroads between Europe, Africa, and Asia that its inhabitants never have had much chance for peace. Often a battleground, usually under foreign rule, the area has only recently emerged into the community of sovereign nations.

The Arab world stretches 3,300 miles from the Atlantic Ocean to the desolate Arab sheikdoms on the Persian Gulf and 1,100 miles from the Euphrates Valley to the sources of the White Nile, deep in the African continent. Of its area of 5,000,000 square miles, 75 percent is composed of deserts and arid mountains. Most of its fertile land lies in a narrow belt paralleling the Mediterranean coast, as do its big cities from Beirut to Algiers. More than 110,000,000 people live there, in the strikingly new apartments of Damascus or in the walled mud-brick cities of Yemen. It is a world of shocking contrasts, of extreme poverty and insolent wealth, of verdant valleys and barren deserts.

37

Ethnically the Middle East—which is part of the Arab world—is a melting pot of Arab, Kurd, Turkoman, Armenian, Jew, Berber, and a score of forgotten peoples. In 1920 Europeans controlled virtually the whole Arab world. By 1967 the British had surrendered control of their strategic base in Aden to the brand-new People's Republic of South Yemen; even the tiny island of Cyprus had long since acquired independence—though fighting between Turks and Greeks continued there.

Such rapid political changes often occurred with violence: Arab nationalism, Greek nationalism, Jewish nationalism alternately played a role in the series of guerrilla wars that marked recent years in the Middle East.

South of the Sahara, the heavy hand of Arab rulers on Negro animists and Christians has resulted in the obscure war of the Sudan where 100,000 have already died. The ugly racial conflict might well spill over to the new republics of Chad and Niger. In the long range, the traditional animosity between Muslim Arabs and black Africans could bring a new wave of racial wars to the African continent, where Islam is attracting millions of non-Arab Africans.

On the massive Arabian Peninsula, the unsettled situation in Yemen, where royalists and republicans are at each other's throats, leaves the door open to all kinds of foreign intervention. After the failure of Arab socialism preached by Egypt's Gamal Abdel Nasser, there is evidence that the Soviets are trying to move in to promote the interests of Russian policy in the Middle East. United States power is no longer predominant in the Mediterranean, already vacated by the French and British fleets.

Because the Arab world is now at the center of world oil production, it will continue to be a factor in the power struggle between East and West. But because of the barren

terrain, the lack of shelter, the scarcity of food, and the low
population density, the fighting will probably continue on
the level of the terrorism in South Yemen rather than on
the model of the guerrilla armies of Southern Asia—unless,
of course, a new explosion erupts between Israel and its
Arab neighbors.

Present U.S. policy is to use diplomatic means to prevent
an arms race in the Arab world and to prevent any nation
from dominating the area.

ALGERIA

Algeria, with a population of about 12,000,000 in 1968, became independent on July 3, 1962, after a bitter seven-year
rebellion against the Paris government, which regarded the
predominantly Muslim country as an integral part of
France. Four times larger than metropolitan France, Algeria
is situated in North Africa, extending 640 miles along the
Mediterranean Sea, between Tunisia on the east and Morocco on the west. Geographically, these three gallicized
countries form the Maghrib (Arabic for "the West"). Once
known as the Granary of Rome, the Maghrib was succes-
sively invaded and fought over by the Romans, Vandals,
Byzantines, Arabs, Spaniards and Ottoman Turks.

By the beginning of the 19th century, the country's once
flourishing agriculture was ruined. Piracy and the slave
trade were a dwindling source of revenues for the Barbary
port. Even the proud *beys* of Algiers were reduced to ruling
Algeria on behalf of the Turkish sultan. In 1827, the last
bey of Algiers called in French Consul Pierre Deval and,
after charging him with being "wicked and faithless,"
struck him three times with a fly whisk. In that insult France
saw an occasion to conquer the Barbary coast and eliminate the privateers who preyed on Western shipping.

Conquest of the country came swiftly, and in 1842 Algiers became part of France. In the ensuing half-century, more than a million impoverished Europeans, only half of them of French descent, settled in Algeria, built ports and cities, and developed its agriculture. Although many Muslim Algerians were lifted from poverty, France refused to grant them full citizenship rights unless they abandoned Muslim practices such as polygamy. Some educated Algerians of the professional class, however, became so gallicized that, to this day, they speak better French than Arabic. All that would have been needed at the beginning to transform Algeria into a true part of France were self-rule and legal equality between Algerian Muslims and Europeans.

The drive for Algeria's independence began on November 1, 1954, when thirty bands of the *Front de Libération Nationale* (FLN) struck at points across the land, killing French soldiers and policemen. Not many were killed in this action—only seven, and so it was that at the beginning, the French dismissed the revolt as an outbreak of terrorism. But as European farms were attacked and their occupants murdered, the French belatedly realized that something was wrong with *l'Algérie française*. Crack French troops freed by the end of the war in Indochina were quickly diverted to Algiers.

Many of the FLN guerrillas were trained in the Kabylia hills by former Algerian noncommissioned officers of the French Army. One was Belkacem Krim, a moody, balding former corporal. Another was Ahmed ben Bella, a former warrant officer who had fought at Monte Cassino. Significantly, the rebellion was fought mainly by the rural Berbers, not by the city-dwelling Arabs. One of its strongholds was the forbidding Aurès mountains, where guerrillas ambushed road convoys, killing French and French-appointed local Muslim officials. The guerrillas took few prisoners; those falling into their hands they often mutilated and killed. The French in turn adopted a policy of violent reprisals against Muslim villages.

By the middle of 1956, some 400,000 French Union troops were tied down in Algeria against 30,000 uniformed rebels and about 100,000 occasional guerrillas, who received support from the country's 7,000,000 rural Muslims. In the following year, to seal off Algeria from Tunisia, French forces began constructing the *Ligne Morice*—a 150-mile electrified barbed-wire fence running from the Mediterranean coast to the fringe of the Sahara desert parallel to the Tunisian frontier. The Morice Line was later expanded to 500 miles, with heavy patrols and batteries of artillery activated by an elaborate detection system and searchlights. The French accused Habib Bourguiba's Tunisia of providing a sanctuary for FLN guerrillas. Algerian guerrillas went to Tunisia for training and returned fully equipped to fight the French.

Along the Moroccan border, French army engineers installed a less sophisticated barrier with minefields and forts. This strategy was partly successful. The 35,000-man FLN army based in Tunisia, though equipped with modern Czech and German weapons, could no longer reinforce the hard-pressed *djounouds* (combatants) inside Algeria.

In October 1956, French counterintelligence agents captured a C-47 aircraft carrying Ben Bella and four other leaders of the rebellion to an FLN war council in Morocco. By that time, FLN terrorists had exploded their first bomb in Algiers, killing a number of Frenchmen indiscriminately. The bomb, followed by murders of pro-French Algerians, signaled the Battle of Algiers.

To deal with the terrorism, the French sent General

Jacques Massu's 10th Airborne Division to Algiers, where the
rebels were planting bombs in movie houses and department stores. The paratroopers took a tight hold on the
labyrinthian Casbah. They mercilessly tortured suspects
until they revealed what they knew of a particular rebel
organization. Couriers—often young girls—carrying mes-
sages for the rebels were arrested with the help of Muslim
defectors and tortured until they confessed the addresses of
their leaders. This French counterterror was effective. The
Muslim organization, helped by European sympathizers,
fell apart. In 1957, Yacef Saadi, the chief of 150 FLN terrorists in Algiers, was captured—and the Battle of Algiers
was ended. The remaining leaders of the FLN fled the city
and took refuge in Tunisia.

The Battle of Algiers was just the beginning. In the fury
of the war that followed, French soldiers such as Colonel
Jean Trinquier argued that torture was a necessary and
legal weapon since the adversary was not respecting the
laws of conventional warfare. There were mopping-up
operations, brutal transfers of population, harsh reprisal
expeditions, and massacres of women and children by air
power and artillery.

The rebels, on their part, showed no mercy whatever
toward anyone suspected of supplying intelligence to the
French. Periodic purges eliminated loyal guerrilla leaders
regarded as dangerous rivals by others. Agents of the FLN,
for example, often betrayed to the French police members
of the rival nationalist organization, the *Mouvement National Algérien* (MNA). French policemen, who had to
torture FLN prisoners to extract information, often became insane under the moral stress.

The FLN was not a party driven by a particular ideology,
but rather a popular front including young intellectuals;

affluent bourgeois, frustrated in their vain search for an entente with France; and hard-bitten terrorists who found in violence an outlet for their extreme nationalism. At bottom was the mass of impoverished peasants resenting the domination of the European *colons* (settlers) and the arrogant *pieds noirs,* the poor whites reluctant to give up their exorbitant privileges. Only the *pieds noirs,* the "black feet," so nicknamed because their ancestors had arrived in Algeria barefoot, possessed such easy government jobs as city policemen or customs inspectors.

The FLN theoretician was the famous black psychoanalyst from Martinique, Dr. Frantz Fanon, who died later of leukemia in the United States. His famous book *The Wretched of the Earth* analyzed in detail the mental frustrations and trauma of a colonized people. Fanon brilliantly argued that physical violence is a psychic experience through which the colonized man must go to kill the oppressor: "The country should be turned over to those who have nothing to lose, the landless peasants who provide the bulk of the fighters and for whom the struggle means only two things—freedom and bread." Fanon was the first student of decolonization to describe the mental disorders arising from wars of national liberation—disorders resulting in terror, torture, psychosis, and loss of humanitarian feeling.

In Algeria, the French army ultimately mustered 450,000 men; almost all the Navy and the Air Force were based there. Governor René Lacoste instituted territorial units 100,000 strong, levied among the *pieds noirs* and, later, urban European militias to assist the police in checking urban terrorism. The repression was systematized and the manhunt organized on a giant scale. Pro-French Arabs were enrolled to provide security to Arab villages regrouped by the French Army in secure areas along the main roads. The 50,000 "professional" troops of the French army, the Legionnaires, the paratroopers, and the commando units, fought well, using with profit their experience acquired in Indochina.

But the young French draftee had no enthusiasm for this endless colonial war; many conscript units lacked aggressiveness; if sent on operations they often blundered into deadly ambushes.

The FLN, too, had its weaknesses. It indulged in fruitless squabbles and rarely carried out nighttime raids against isolated French outposts. Trained by former French army noncommissioned officers, the FLN army adopted many of the French mannerisms, including a taste for flashy uniforms and bureaucracy.

The strongholds of the FLN rebellion were the mountains, the impoverished Kabylia region of eastern Algeria, the formidable range of the Aurès mountains, and half a dozen pockets of insecurity along the coast and along the Moroccan frontier. The basic unit of the *Armée de Libération Nationale* (ALN) was the company-size *Katiba* of 90 to 150 regulars responsible for the local *moussebilines* (guerrillas and guides) of its area.

The rebels divided Algeria into six military regions, each subdivided in districts, subdistricts, and cells. The colonels commanding the politico-military structures were the most important men in the rebellion, receiving their orders directly from the nine top leaders, who commuted between Cairo, Tunis, and Switzerland. Each unit commander was considered a political-military representative of the FLN's central authority. The "external" leadership collected funds, carried terrorism to metropolitan France, recruited supporters among European intellectuals, brought the Algerian question to the United Nations, and, later, organized the self-proclaimed Provisional Government of the Algerian Republic.

In the name of Algerian nationalism the provisional government waged a successful political and diplomatic war against Paris. Of course, Egypt's Gamal Abdel Nasser did his best to assist the Algerian rebels. But, regarding themselves as Algerians first and Arabs second, the rebels were not always grateful for Nasser's efforts.

France's career soldiers in Algeria were obsessed with the idea of proving that they could defeat an insurgency using guerrilla tactics they had learned from their defeat in Indochina. To the command of Algeria, Premier Charles de Gaulle—himself brought to power by a revolt of French generals and right-wing settlers in Algiers—appointed Air Force General Maurice Challes. A squat, quiet man, Challes produced a plan under which crack army units were removed from fixed posts and sent marauding into the mountains to ferret out the rebels.

Under the Challes Plan, a classic of counterguerrilla warfare, the French army was to (1) close the frontiers to infiltrators; (2) destroy the large FLN battalions and fragment them into smaller units; (3) uproot the enemy political-administrative infrastructure among the populace; and (4) install a native pro-French administration in the villages. Challes concentrated his crack mobile forces against the four major FLN strongholds. Each one, treated separately, was isolated by a belt of French-manned outposts. Then the area was saturated with infantry battalions assigned to evacuate all civilian populations, and to destroy crops and *mechtas* (houses) used by the guerrillas during the bitter cold winter in the mountains.

To track each rebel *Katiba,* Challes assigned a French Muslim *Commando de Chasse* (Hunting Company), whose role was to carry out long-range patrols in the countryside, to gather intelligence, and always to keep contact with the FLN unit. Flushed out of their hideouts, the rebels sought refuge in mountain caves, often reduced to a meager diet because the peasants could no longer provide them with food. Meanwhile, the French Army carried on massive psychological warfare to persuade the ordinary Arab to become a loyal French citizen, "because France alone has the resources to modernize Algeria."

Civil affairs officers of the French Army brought some education and medical care to Arab villages that accepted French protection. New roads were built, new oil fields were exploited, and an ambitious plan for industrialization was laid out. To isolate the guerrillas, 2,000,000 peasants were uprooted from their villages and crowded into resettlement centers; another 500,000 fled to *bidonvilles* (shantytowns) on the outskirts of the prosperous cities. The Challes Plan was relatively successful: from a high of 100,000 guerrillas, the rebels were brought down to 15,000. But the war was expensive, and an annual $600,000,000 was siphoned out of the French economy.

The Algerian rebels had lost the contest with the French Army, but they had won the political battle. The army controlled Algeria but could not install an effective native government enjoying the active support of the majority of the population. Furthermore, the Algerian war had resulted in a crippling diplomatic isolation of France. These factors finally induced Charles de Gaulle to open negotiations with the fifty-four members of the Algerian National Revolutionary Council. The talks lasted nine months.

The French no longer opposed Algeria's independence

but refused to give way on key issues: continued French access to the Sahara oil, guarantees for European minorities living in Algeria (eventually they decided to emigrate), and use of the Sahara for French nuclear testing. In exchange, Paris agreed to continue its economic and cultural assistance to the new Algerian republic and to open the doors of France to Algerian workers. The French Army was given a generous five years for a gradual pull-out from Algeria. Brokenhearted, the Foreign Legion evacuated its headquarters at Sidi-bel-Abbès.

In March 1962 after seven years, four months, and 18 days, the fighting stopped. The war had cost an estimated 380,000 lives, of whom 2,000 were European settlers, 18,000 French army soldiers, 16,000 FLN guerrillas, and at least 200,000 Muslim civilians. It had sparked two mutinies in the French army, destroyed the Fourth Republic, brought to power the Fifth Republic of Charles de Gaulle, and seriously undermined his regime, too.

AFTERMATH OF THE ALGERIAN WAR

The war's cruelty and the revelation of outrages against FLN prisoners caused a painful crisis of conscience among intellectuals in France, who opposed the conflict and encouraged desertions among French draftees. De Gaulle himself was accused of selling out French interests and of abandoning 1,000,000 countrymen who called Algeria their motherland. As news of the cease-fire reached Algiers, a new French war had already started—against General Raoul Salan's fanatical Secret Army Organization, dedicated to the use of terror to remove de Gaulle, by assassination, if necessary.

In April 1961, four retired French generals headed by former Air Force Chief Maurice Challes—but recently Gen-

eral Charles de Gaulle's commander in Algeria—led an
army mutiny against the Paris government. Other leaders
were Generals Jean Jouhaud and Raoul Salan, who commanded French armies in Indochina and Algeria. The
mutiny, supported by 1,000,000 European settlers, was triggered by de Gaulle's willingness to grant independence to
Algeria. To the old battle-cry *"Algérie Française,"* the *pieds
noirs* of Oran and Algiers took to the streets to cheer the
three paratroop regiments that seized power in Algiers.

In four days the new revolt was in shreds, mainly because
the 350,000 French army conscripts in North Africa did not
share the zeal of the 50,000 professional soldiers who were
determined to keep Algeria French. Maurice Challes surrendered, but Jouhaud, Salan, and scores of other prestigious French officers led by Colonels Yves Godard, Antoine
Argoud, and Gardes, went underground to form the *Organ-
isation de l'Armée Secrète* (OAS). The tactics of the OAS
were borrowed from Mao Tse-tung's theories on revolutionary warfare, which had made a strong impression on
French officers fighting in Indochina. First, strong psychological pressure would be brought to bear on the local
population to achieve collaboration. Second, to further this
end, the army would become involved with every aspect of
the community's life, living with the people "like a fish in
water." Many of the younger French officers advocated land
reform and sweeping social changes to "integrate" the
Arabs into the French community.

The OAS had plenty of men to use, mainly deserters who
were ready to assassinate—for a price—anyone named by
the organization either for favoring de Gaulle or for re-
fusing to pay financial tribute. Plastic bombs were exploded
nightly in Algiers. Arabs were killed indiscriminately, simply to frighten the Muslim population into submission.

But the main targets of the OAS Delta Squads were the French *barbouzes* (the bearded ones), the secret service policemen sent by de Gaulle to put down the OAS. The *barbouzes* captured Jouhaud and then Salan, who were sentenced to life imprisonment. These two men were held responsible for 1,800 murders, 4,700 people wounded, and 12,000 armed attacks, and countless bank robberies to provide funds for the OAS. When they realized that the independence of Algeria was inevitable, the remaining OAS leaders decided to transfer their terrorist methods to metropolitan France and to wage guerrilla war against the government.

The regrouping of the OAS leaders on the European mainland took place around the figures of former Premier Georges Bidault and former Gaullist Minister Jacques Soustelle, both of whom had sworn to overthrow de Gaulle's regime. Calling themselves the "Council of National Resistance," the two dissident politicians met with OAS military leaders to plan an all-out attempt to seize power in France. From his hideout in Italy Colonel Argoud plotted several attempts on de Gaulle's life. In one of these, known as the Petit Clamart affair, OAS marksmen riddled de Gaulle's Citroën with bullets. Then Argoud was kidnapped in Germany by counterespionage agents of the French. Colonel Godard, former chief of the military and civilian intelligence in Algiers, took over.

The OAS terrorists in metropolitan France were small in numbers—only about 600—but they were fanatically dedicated, and they could count on support among the 800,000 Algerian French who poured into France after 1961. Some 30,000 others, even more hostile to de Gaulle, chose to settle in Spain. Their last hope was that de Gaulle's removal would bring political chaos followed by an army coup against the Fifth Republic to restore order. The establishment of a right-wing, authoritarian government would have been the end result. In fact, the OAS enjoyed the sympathy of many French career officers who had never forgiven de Gaulle's "betrayal" in Algeria, nor his decision to pull out the army from its overseas garrisons.

The outside world never quite realized how close the OAS men came to seizing power in France. For two years following Algeria's independence, the entire French police force was mobilized to fight the OAS. Eventually, more than 3,000 OAS affiliates were arrested. Among them were aristocratic officers such as Lieutenant Colonel Jean-Marie Bastien-Thiry, a graduate of the topnotch École Polytechnique, on whom de Gaulle himself had conferred the Cross of the Legion of Honor. Arrested after the Petit Clamart road ambush, Bastien-Thiry was sentenced to death and executed by a firing squad. Captain George Watin, the sharpshooter who had sprayed de Gaulle's limousine with 150 bullets, was never caught. Still at large also are Jo Ortiz, the fiery leader of the *pieds noirs* who launched the Barricades Revolt in Algiers in January 1960, and Colonel Pierre Château Robert, another renegade officer who has escaped the legendary triggermen of the French secret service.

The OAS failure was partly due to the refusal of the majority of Frenchmen to be intimidated by strong-arm tactics. French public opinion was tired of costly colonial wars in faraway places and was generally behind de Gaulle's decision to terminate the Algerian conflict.

De Gaulle brought the restive French army back under control by purging right-wing officers from the Foreign Legion and from airborne units whose *esprit de corps* and adventurism could easily have been turned against him. A generous policy was later adopted toward former OAS

sympathizers; those who desired to return and live peace-
fully in France were helped financially. Only 17 of them
would remain in French jails.

An interesting footnote: It was the liberal French intellectuals of the left—such as Jean Paul Sartre—who were the
first to protest the Algerian war. Later, they courageously
denounced the OAS attempt to transfer its bloodletting and
brutality onto the soil of metropolitan France.

TUNISIA'S HABIB BOURGUIBA
"I hate colonialism, not the French."
Habib Bourguiba

Tunisia's recent history and struggle for independence from
France is closely identified with the career of Habib Bourguiba, a Paris-educated lawyer who became known to his
4,000,000 countrymen as *Mujahid Akbar,* the Supreme
Combatant.

Caught in history's traditional dilemma between his
Western education, his taste for French humanities, and his
people's national consciousness, Habib Bourguiba, born on
August 3, 1903, gradually developed a love-hate relationship
toward France as he emerged as an Arab nationalist. Like
many of North Africa's new leaders, the blue-eyed Bourguiba is more literate in French than in Arabic and feels
more at home culturally in a French atmosphere than in an
Islamic one. (He persuaded modern Tunisian women to
abandon the veil and abolished the tradition allowing any
Muslim male to "own" seven wives.)

As a dynamic, handsome, well-tailored young lawyer,
Bourguiba married a French woman he had met in Paris
and after practicing law in Tunis for a while, became active
in politics in 1930. A fiery nationalist, he organized the
broad-based Neo-Destour (Constitution) Party with cells

in 100 Tunisian villages and cities. The two-phase aims of the Neo-Destour were first, to obtain internal autonomy from France, and second, to achieve complete independence and sovereignty.

For the next twenty-five years, Paris adamantly refused even to discuss the question of independence. Regarded as a dangerous, Marxist-influenced agitator by the French, Bourguiba spent eleven years in jail or in exile. During World War II, he resisted efforts by the Germans and the Italians to secure from him a declaration in support of Axis aims. Because of the presence of an important Italian minority (85,000 persons) in Tunisia, Rome had revived an old Italian claim on Tunisia. But Bourguiba, an astute politician, was not prepared to trade French colonialism for Italian fascism.

In 1945 the creation of the Arab League brought marked assistance and encouragement to the Neo-Destour. Bourguiba then set up a new program for the party. In Tunisia it would seek to expand its influence among youth and in labor and business circles through satellite organizations; and create paramilitary forces to rouse the enthusiasm of young Tunisians for the goal of independence. Abroad, the Neo-Destour was to establish relations with progressive French politicians and parties among whom supporters for the cause of Tunisia's independence could be enlisted.

Even more important, Bourguiba realized that by constantly alerting international public opinion and the United Nations to the Tunisian problem he would embarrass France diplomatically and bring pressure to bear on the Paris government. At home, a detailed agitation plan put into action by the Neo-Destour resulted in incidents, rioting, and demonstrations against the French authorities in Tunis. The scattered terrorist attempts triggered a ruthless

French repression. In one case, thousands of Foreign Legionnaires were sent to "mop up" Arab villages in the Cape Bon Peninsula.

This action increased the anti-French sentiment among the Tunisian public. The Neo-Destour affirmed itself as a party with a popular cause and the support of a broad cross-section of the population, from unschooled Berber camel drivers to the sophisticated urban élite who until then had identified themselves with the French. A rather peaceable people, the Tunisians had to be aroused by a messianic leader such as Bourguiba to become convinced of the necessity of challenging the French.

Once popular support had been mustered to back their cause, the Neo-Destour leaders gave the signal for armed opposition to the French. Parallel to the action of clandestine groups in urban centers, armed bands of *fellaghas* went into action in the countryside and gradually became active over vast chunks of territory, fostering everywhere an atmosphere of insecurity and unrest. Two organizations were then created to coordinate the operations: A civilian one headquartered in Tunis recruited, supplied, and financed the *fellaghas*. The other, military and based in Tripoli (Libya), trained and indoctrinated political cadres for the anti-French movement at home.

In March 1954 the French government offered partial self-government for Tunisia, but the proposal was rejected as insufficient. Terrorist activities of the *fellaghas* spread throughout the country. Recruiting of new members was actively pursued, and the number of guerrillas increased rapidly. Within three months, the *fellaghas* extended their influence over the southern part of the country where the French army—still bogged down in Indochina—could send only skeleton units to fight an elusive enemy.

Under the overall leadership of Habib Bourguiba and Salah ben Youssef, the secretary general of the Neo-Destour, the party carried on a truly revolutionary war, concurrently using psychological and political means, terrorist activities and diplomacy, legal and illegal forms of political struggle, to keep alive the cause of Tunisian independence. By the end of 1954, the French *résident-général* in Tunisia agreed that full amnesty be granted to all the *fellaghas* who surrendered and turned over their weapons. Almost all the rebels, about 2,500 men, accepted the offer.

Bourguiba returned triumphantly from exile when France granted Tunisia internal autonomy in 1955. He became premier a year later and assumed the presidency when Tunisia proclaimed itself a republic in July 1957. His overriding concern then became the preservation of Tunisia's relations with France. He decided against following the path of Arab neutralism and socialism set by Nasser, and he allowed the French to maintain some 22,000 troops on Tunisian soil in ten bases, including the great naval base of Bizerte, until 1963. This moderate policy led to a split with Salah ben Youssef, who described it as pro-French. But Youssef was forced to leave the country; years later he was assassinated in West Germany, after failure of his efforts to revive the *fellagha* movement against Bourguiba—with Egyptian help.

YEMEN

In September 1962 came word of a palace revolution that had toppled the dynasty of Imam Mohammed al-Badr, who had just succeeded his father, Imam Ahmad, called "the Devil," as Imam of Yemen. The leader of the coup was Colonel Abdullah al-Salal, newly appointed commander of the palace guard. The stern, heavy-set Salal announced in Şan'ā, the capital, that his troops had killed the young Imam and were in control of the fiefdom. Only weeks later was it learned that the Imam (a title given to a prince exercising spiritual as well as temporal leadership over a Muslim region) had escaped the ruins of his palace and found refuge in Yemen's forbidding hill country, whose warlike tribes have traditionally been loyal to their religious ruler.

Salal immediately proclaimed himself president of the new republic of Yemen. His support came mainly from young officers and from wealthy expatriates who had resented the old feudal system imposed by despotic Arab sheiks over their country. To prop up his regime, President Salal made the mistake of calling upon Egypt's Gamal Abdel Nasser, who immediately sensed an opportunity in the situation for jabs at his implacable foes, the immensely rich sheiks of Saudi Arabia. Ever since he had assumed power in Egypt, Nasser had dreamed of bringing the oil-producing kingdoms, sultanates, and emirates of Arabia under the influence of his expansionist United Arab Republic. Because of its position near the British base of Aden, Yemen was also an advantageous place to start aiming blows at British influence in the region.

Weeks after the republican coup, Imam Mohammed—a tough, turbaned Arab sporting a decorative bandoleer across his chest and a curved, wide-bladed *djambias* (dagger) thrust into his belt—began to rally his supporters for a reconquest of his throne. Mohammed and his nephew, Prince Abdullah, had mustered enough ragtag Yemenite tribesmen around them to carry on resistance against the Egyptian army. Both Saudi Arabia and Jordan, opposed to any penetration of Nasser's Arab socialism into their area, pledged aid to Mohammed and his royalist supporters.

Until 1965, it appeared that Salal and his Egyptian allies would succeed in subduing the royalist tribes. The republican military power was overwhelming, and Salal safely held the richer coastal areas.

With massive foreign assistance the regime was building new schools and Yemen's first industrial plants. For the first time in Yemen's history, some 70,000 children were attending school. Because of a lack of qualified Yemenites, the school system was run by Egyptians, who numbered about 200. Another 2,000 Egyptians served as advisers, superseding at all levels the outdated Yemenite administration, including the prison system; enemies of the republican regime were jailed in increasing numbers. Although the republicans did not control more than half of the country, the United States had decided in December 1962 to recognize Salal's regime and to extend economic assistance for a much-needed irrigation system.

As the threat of a royalist counteroffensive in the barren hinterland became more serious, Nasser rushed in 23,000 Egyptian troops. Their T-44 tanks, Soviet-made guns, and MIG jets made them a formidable fighting force against the barefooted tribes equipped with old rifles and with only camels and donkeys for transport. The Egyptians had thousands of trucks to move their troops quickly and observation aircraft to ferret out the royalists' movements on the trails. Gradually, Nasser raised his expeditionary corps to 40,000, then to 50,000 men.

Salal's reliance on the disliked Egyptians, who bombed and strafed Yemenite villages and herds indiscriminately, made him increasingly unpopular with the tribes. Gradually he abdicated his shaky authority to Egyptian advisers, who ran Yemen as a protectorate. For Egypt, it was a costly adventure.

Civil war persisted. Harold Vocke, a German correspondent for a Frankfurt paper, reported after a visit to Yemen:

"Egyptian troops decide what happens in republican Yemen. The backbone of the republican army consists of Yemenites trained in Egypt, the Soviet Union, and Czechoslovakia. This is because the large warrior tribes are no longer willing to fight for the republican government. Not a single minister in the Salal cabinet has any influence on the tribes. Yet there are still tribes in the south who knuckle under. The authority of the republicans is ineffective in their region, and they pay no taxes to Salal's regime. But they have bought their freedom from air attacks with lip service to the republic. In spite of this, the Egyptian occupation army feels threatened in the deep south of Yemen—even in the southern province, whose population, like the Egyptian Muslims, belong to the Sunnite branch of Islam and do not regard the Imam Mohammed as their religious leader. The towns in this province once greeted the Egyptians as liberators."

In 1965 the royalists counterattacked on Red Mountain, inflicting severe losses on Egyptian columns. To avoid their fall to the royalists, the Egyptians had to pull out their isolated military outposts on the northern plateau. Truces were periodically negotiated in Beirut or Khartoum, only to be violated by both sides before the ink had dried on the documents. Nasser repeatedly promised to withdraw his army, but feared to keep his word lest the republican regime collapse.

The border town of Najran, in Saudi Arabia, became the royalists' main camp and supply base. There, some 100 French mercenaries led by the enigmatic Major Roger Faulques trained 3,000 royalists in the art of firing heavy mortars and bazookas. Radio communications were provided by a sizable number of Arabic-speaking British secret agents disguised as Bedouins. Reportedly, they received their orders from a mysterious London headquarters called "The

Organization." A publicity-shy German known as Dr. Herbert Stolz managed a broadcasting station for the Imam. All the modern equipment was buried in grottoes.

The fighting was most intense in an 80-mile arc around the approaches to Ṣanʻā, where Salal lived under Egyptian protection. In some areas, the royalists limited themselves to hit-and-run guerrilla raids. Elsewhere, they attacked along a broad front and kept advancing steadily. In many regions, the tribesmen held the mountains while the Egyptians controlled the low ground with their tanks and their superior firepower. Egyptian soldiers from the Nile valley were ill-suited for this sort of 12th-century war. Restricted to the few rugged roads, the Egyptians depended upon regular supplies, whereas the royalists could travel anywhere with a bandoleer of cartridges, a loaf of hard bread, and *qat,* a narcotic leaf chewed to dull hunger.

The Egyptian strategy was to isolate and starve the royalists, whose meager crops and herds of camels were devastated by air attacks. Periodically, the royalist north was famine-stricken, and perhaps as many as 100,000 Yemenites died. Yet the frustrated Egyptians discovered that with a handful of gold coins the Imam could sway a whole tribe to the royalist cause.

Nasser's many words about socialism were little understood. Many Yemenites were plainly delighted by this occasion to indulge in their favorite pastimes: making war, and remaining poor, hungry, and free. The situation in Yemen was costly and inglorious for Nasser. His protégé Salal became a haunted man on the verge of a nervous breakdown; repeatedly he was flown to Cairo for treatment. A 200-man United Nations team, composed mostly of Yugoslav soldiers and Canadian airmen, was sent in to stop the fighting, but it was too small to police the vast Yemeni frontier. The peace attempt failed, and the ugly guerrilla war continued.

In 1967, in the wake of Egypt's disastrous defeat during the six-day war with Israel, Nasser was forced to curtail his military commitment in Yemen. For many reasons, Nasser and also the British in Aden were becoming disenchanted with their involvement in the region. After Great Britain officially announced that it would withdraw from South Arabia and let the warring local factions settle their own affairs, Nasser encouraged the republican Yemenites to seek negotiations with royalist tribal leaders. In November, at an Arab summit conference in Khartoum, Nasser reached an accord on Yemen with King Faisal of Saudi Arabia. Shortly afterward, Nasser began to pull his troops out of Yemen—five years after their ill-fated commitment to a guerrilla war that cost Egypt millions of dollars and added little to Nasser's prestige.

This is not, of course, the end of the story—or of the civil war. At the Khartoum meeting at the end of August 1967, a 3-nation committee was set up (Iraq, Morocco, Sudan) to try to solve the problem in Yemen—it was not agreed to by Salal (parallel to Diem's attitude in Vietnam!). In November Salal—on a visit to Iraq—was deposed. In December the royalists began a siege of Ṣanʿā, which was broken in February 1968. Royalists said the Chinese had helped the republicans by building roads. Faisal said on February 28 he would resume his help to the royalists. Meanwhile, the three-nation committee had met in January and had been unable to get the two sides to confer.

ADEN: ARABIAN NIGHTMARE FOR THE BRITISH
From 1962, when the Federation of South Arabia was formed from a conglomeration of pocket-sized Arab states,

the traditionalist sheiks and sultans had looked askance at the prospect of federation with politically restive Aden. In 1967, the British announcement of early withdrawal from Aden immediately triggered a bitter struggle for power among the bickering Arab political factions, some supported by Egypt, others by Saudi Arabia. Soon, the seething city of Aden became an arena for competing Arab terrorists.

In the hinterland, rival bands of guerrillas fought for control of tiny sultanates. To compound the disorder, Arab officers of the British-trained South Arabian army mutinied. By midyear it was clear that the British dream of a peaceable South Arabian federation had evaporated under the scorching desert sun. British forces were involved in a guerrilla war on the desolate shores of the Red Sea.

The political problems of Aden and the adjacent South Arabian areas were much more than a localized struggle for power. The conflict between Arab socialism and Arab traditionalism was entangled with larger power considerations, and the reason is that Aden stands at a strategic crossroads. The port looks northeast to the oil-rich Persian Gulf while commanding the southern entrance to the Red Sea.

The struggle for control of Aden and South Arabia had gone on for five years. Two powerful terrorist groups—the Front for the Liberation of Occupied South Yemen (FLOSY) and the National Liberation Front (NLF)— were waging war among the 300,000 fear-stricken inhabitants. The Secretary General of FLOSY had publicly stated his party's determination to engage in "all-out armed revolutionary struggle."

Containing terrorism in Aden and elsewhere in South Arabia entailed enormous problems for Great Britain. The 2,500 men of its Aden Brigade encountered a particularly vicious type of urban terrorism—bomb blasts and gunfire in the streets, grenade attacks on women and children, and bazooka blasts on families of British servicemen. John Soak, a British journalist, reported: "Kid-glove treatment of the population has won no support. Terrorists regard restraint as weakness and take full advantage. Escaping terrorists rush for crowds, knowing that the soldiers will not risk a shot, hide in mosques, and traverse Aden under the veil of Muslim women."

Strict control of the Aden border reduced arms smuggling, but handling terrorists in a city consisting of ancient warrens, shanties, and numerous small apartments was an almost impossible task. The basic antiterrorist strategy consisted of assigning a sector of Aden City to each battalion, with a Joint Security Center in charge of curfew, reinforcements, imposition of area-wide roadblocks, and assignment of helicopters.

In his Security Center, the duty controller played a game of chess with the terrorists. If a suspect vehicle broke through a checkpoint, for instance, the duty controller maneuvered his armored cars to set up the net in which to catch the terrorist.

The hours of duty were arduous, but the off-duty hours were little easier. A turbulent riot situation was routine, and soldiers had to catch brief periods of rest on the floor of police barracks, hating every hour of their two-year tour of duty in Aden.

Fifty miles east of Aden was another world, in which the traditional structure of Arab society was unimpaired. It was a wild land of jagged peaks, fiercely hot sands, and fortress-like dwellings situated on hilltops. The people in the tribal area were warriors and individualists to whom the concepts of Arab socialism were alien.

The Federal Regular Army (FRA) operated in this out-lying area, where paved roads were virtually nonexistent. Organized into five battalions, the units were made up of hill Arabs recruited fairly equally among the tribal components of the Federation. Commanded by Arabs, not by British officers as in former times, they moved lightly clad, wearing gym shoes, and seemed to dance over the rough hill country, keeping their rifles balanced flat on their shoulders.

By the end of 1967, the idea of a South Arabian Federation was definitively shelved as Britain accelerated plans to leave. The British had hoped to turn power over to the National Liberation Front, which had won the support of the Federation's 9,000-man army and which represented the de facto authority in Aden. But as NLF President Qahtan al-Shaabi prepared to discuss final arrangements for independence, the rival FLOSY threatened to contest the take-over with violence. Finally, the British rearguard departed, forty days earlier than the date set by London for independence. This ended 129 years of British presence in Aden.

What happened in Aden is a case history of terror: The Arabs waged a classic terrorist campaign, ruthless and absolutely perfect, and they achieved their ends: creation of a genuine popular revolution and expulsion of the British.

In November 1967, the new nation became known as the People's Republic of South Yemen, with Qahtan al-Shaabi as president. As one American on the scene grimly remarked, "South Arabia had no independence-day ball. There were still too many gunmen around."

UNITED STATES INTERVENTION IN LEBANON

Behind the Lebanese revolt, whether he started it or not, was Egypt's Gamal Abdel Nasser, whose cry for *Al Umma al Arabia* (Arab unity) and fiery brand of militant socialism sent shock waves from Cairo to Baghdad. In May 1958, the decision of Lebanese President Camille Chamoun to seek a second six-year term triggered a revolt by pro-Nasser rebels. Chamoun, a Catholic of the Maronite sect (as the President of Lebanon is required by custom to be), could not rely on his Defense Minister, the cautious General Fouad Chehab, for support against the rebels. Chehab was unwilling to risk turning the internal political struggle into a religious war between Christians and Arabs dedicated to making Lebanon a Muslim-run country tied to Egypt.

The leader of the revolt in Beirut was Saeb Salaam, former prime minister and a graduate of the American University of Beirut. His well-armed forces held whole chunks of Lebanese territory, particularly along the border with Syria, whence Egyptian agents smuggled weapons. Muslim rebels were reportedly receiving instructions by telephone from Damascus, and Syrian agents had instigated the riots in Tripoli that triggered the civil war. Egyptian infiltrators had made contact with another rebel leader, Kamam Jumblatt, who had established headquarters near the ancient city of Baalbek. The mountains towering over Beirut offered perfect terrain for guerrilla warfare.

Fearing that the Nasserites would topple the pro-Western Lebanese regime, the United States intervened. Beirut was napping in the midday sun, its rebel leaders out to lunch, when troopships of the U.S. 6th Fleet landed a force of Marines on the beach. They quickly captured Beirut International Airport, where they were met by ice-cream and soda-pop vendors. Not a shot had been fired.

The U.S. intervention convinced the Lebanese warring factions that they would have to compromise if the troops were not to stay indefinitely. Within three months Lebanese deputies convened in parliament to elect a new head of state; even those who had joined the rebellion and were sought by the police showed up under special safe conducts. As President, the parliament elected Defense Minister Fouad Chehab, who quickly reaffirmed Lebanese neutrality in the Arab world. Two months later, the United States withdrew its 12,000-man landing force. The five-month guerrilla sniping had cost 50 dead on both sides.

THE EOKA STRUGGLE IN CYPRUS

"The methods we used were surprise, stratagem, and ruse, and our tactics consisted in dealing the enemy hard and carefully prepared blows of small duration, followed by rapid disengagement and a period of complete tranquillity in the area."

Colonel George Grivas

The British put a price on his head, and for four years some 40,000 British troops combed the small island searching for him. In many places they found evidences of his presence— a booby trap on a trail, a bloody ambush along a road, a defiant poster, a body of a slain informer. But nowhere did the British find Colonel George Grivas, chief of the Greek Cypriot underground organization called EOKA. The British sometimes even wondered whether the elusive George Grivas existed at all.

A mite-size, graying, gaunt man with a bushy mustache, George Grivas was born in 1898 in Cyprus. Educated in Nicosia and at the Military Academy in Athens, he continued his military studies in France. A staff officer of the 2nd Division when German and Italian forces invaded and occupied Greece, he joined the underground and organized a resistance group known simply as *Xhi*. Alongside the British, it first fought the Nazis and then the Communists in the Greek civil war of 1947-49. After an unsuccessful campaign for election to parliament as a right-wing candidate, Grivas began to think of doing something about British rule in Cyprus.

The seeds of trouble in Cyprus had been sown 400 years earlier, when Ottoman Turkey conquered the predominantly Greek island. With the decline of the Ottoman Empire, the Greek Cypriots began agitating for *enosis* (union with Greece), but in 1878 Turkey chose instead to surrender the island to Great Britain. The British maintained vital military bases in Cyprus but did little to develop the island's resources. Although Cyprus lies a bare 40 miles from the Turkish coast, 80 percent of its 600,000 inhabitants are of Greek origin, and less than 20 percent are Muslim Turkish.

After conducting two personal reconnaissances of the island, Grivas made careful plans for his liberation campaign. A meticulous organizer, he left nothing to chance. For example, for months he ate nothing but citrus fruits, he trained himself physically for the hardships to come, and he destroyed all his old clothes so no British scout dog could get a scent from them.

The first phase of Grivas' plan lasted from June 1951 to November 1954, three years during which Grivas drew up his "General Plan of Insurrectionary Action in Cyprus," making arrangements in the island for reception of arms to be sent clandestinely from Greece.

The second phase began with Grivas' secret arrival in Cyprus. Under the name Dighenis, a legendary Greek hero, Grivas devoted five months to organizing and training the first EOKA combat units, to selecting and scouting the first targets, and to drawing plans for attack. Though Grivas wore a quasi-uniform—brown sweater, tan beret, brown pants, and polished boots, a .45 revolver on his hip, and binoculars slung across his chest—for a long time the British did not even suspect his presence on the island.

To this day, Grivas insists that perfect secrecy was the factor that saved the EOKA movement from total failure. Later he was to write, ". . . had the British got wind of what we were doing during the preparatory stage, it would have been impossible to transport the arms to the island . . . and the struggle, even if it broke out at all, would have been nipped in the bud. . . . Careful preparation and securing the element of surprise are half the secret of success. The other half depends on skillful leadership. In my opinion, given these two factors, numbers are not of such importance in guerrilla warfare. . . . The British army in Cyprus was a clumsy weapon completely lacking in the training necessary for this kind of fighting."

Once in Cyprus, Grivas spent much of the time hiding in a tiny cave dug into the side of a hill, its entrance plugged with foliage, a tube running outside for fresh air. To a few trusted friends he confided the strategic conception of his campaign. "By deeds of heroism and self-sacrifice, we will draw the attention of international public opinion.

"By continuously harassing the British in Cyprus, we must show that we are firmly determined not to yield, whatever the sacrifice . . . until the British are compelled to examine the Cyprus problem in accordance with the aspirations of the Cypriot people."

While he trained his little guerrilla army, Grivas warned his supporters that they should not expect to impose total defeat on the British forces in Cyprus. "Our purpose," he stressed repeatedly, "is to win a moral victory through a process of attrition, by harassing, confusing, and finally exasperating the enemy forces."

At first, Grivas concentrated his main effort on sabotage of British installations. The nature of the terrain did not lend itself to a large-scale guerrilla campaign, nor could the small island absorb large guerrilla forces, which would have difficulty hiding or escaping in the event of attack. The terrain, explained Grivas, should at all times appear empty in order to frustrate British search parties, despite their use of scout dogs, helicopters, and observation aircraft.

Though a steely military man by training, Grivas realized that the degree of involvement of the population in the resistance movement would finally decide the outcome. "A revolutionary movement and a guerrilla war in particular," Grivas told friends, "stand no chance of success, whatever the qualities of their leaders, unless they've the complete and unreserved support of the majority of the country's inhabitants. It is toward the civilian population that the movement will turn for assistance of every kind—cadres, fighters, hiding places, equipment, liaison agents, propaganda, intelligence, food, and financial contributions." Bearing in mind that civilians constitute the rear of a guerrilla army, Grivas devoted his attention to organizing the population, not only to involve it actively in the struggle but also to prepare it for long and tough trials—for a guerrilla struggle is above all a matter of time and endurance.

By August 1955, Grivas had brought into action a few groups of guerrillas, but weapons were in short supply, and the guerrillas were forced to use hunting rifles confiscated from their owners. These special detachments called Shotgun Commandos were highly successful in ambushes. Additional munitions were smuggled from Greece by parcel post, or they were manufactured locally, as were land mines and grenades. In this way, under fantastically adverse conditions, Grivas gradually succeeded in forming an invisible army of a few hundred dedicated men eager to get even with the British, who had foolishly embarked on a policy of harsh reprisals against the Cypriots.

The more harshly the British enforced their measures of "population control," the stronger grew the hatred of Greek Cypriots of all classes and ages. Grivas was later to say that Greek Cypriots should one day erect a statue to British Field Marshal Sir John Harding, "for his cruelty and stubbornness helped me more than anything else." Harding was replaced in December 1957 by Sir Hugh Foot, a quite different man and a diplomat, who understood that Britain's way out of the Cyprus predicament lay in appeasement, negotiation, and accommodation with Archbishop Makarios, rather than in a blood bath. But it took four long years to reach that stage.

For the political part of the liberation campaign, Grivas could rely on Archbishop Makarios, whose strong moral authority helped persuade the Orthodox Church of Cyprus to take an active lead in the movement for independence. For centuries the bishops of Cyprus have been the recognized leaders of the nation. For this reason, the alliance between General Grivas and the intractable Makarios was a formidable obstacle to British plans to retain sovereignty over the strategically located island. From March 1956 to April 1957, Makarios and his colleague the Bishop of Kyrenia were exiled to the remote Seychelles Islands, in the Indian Ocean. For a year terrorism raged throughout Cyprus.

The British were unable to grasp the motives that had impelled the Cypriots to rise against them, and to the end they dealt with EOKA members as if they were bandits or terrorists.

Eventually, almost every Greek in Cyprus became an ardent member of the EOKA, although a few renegades cooperated with the British as informers. In the villages, Greek women stoned British troops who came searching for EOKA members. Young girls carried out dangerous missions of liaison and transport of arms. "National liberation movements," said Grivas, "must express the will of the whole people. Liberation struggles succeed only when they find a response among the people."

Interestingly, the weak and isolated Communist leadership in Cyprus dissociated itself totally from the EOKA's struggle and even cooperated with the British. The Communists were unwilling to support a liberation movement, however popular, led by a right-wing general and an orthodox bishop who had no use for Communist class warfare.

By the time Makarios was released from exile, the Turkish community of Cyprus was thoroughly aroused at the prospect of *enosis* (union with Greece) and demanded that the island be partitioned. Cyprus became a three-way quarrel among Greeks, Turks, and British, with Grivas and his Cypriot terrorists keeping alive the flames of revolt. The breakthrough came in the autumn of 1958, when Makarios proposed that after a fixed period of self-government Cyprus should become an independent state. This suggestion eventually led to negotiations between the Greek and Turkish governments in February 1959. In March, Archbishop Makarios persuaded Grivas to lay down his arms and to return to Greece. Ironically, Grivas had spent the better part of the last two years of the insurrection in the port city of Limassol, right under the noses of 200 British intelligence men.

REVOLT OF THE KURDS

"There are three plagues in the world: the rat, the locust, and the Kurd."   (Old Arabian proverb)

"A camel is not an animal, and an Arab is not a human being."   (Old Kurdish proverb)

Since September 1961, the 5,000,000 Kurdish tribesmen of northern Iraq have been conducting open warfare against the Baghdad government, demanding an autonomous state of Kurdistan and many other concessions. To the government of Baghdad the response has been simple: If the Kurds cannot be talked into submission, crush them. The trouble is that the Kurds, who trace their ancestry to the Assyrians in 660 B.C., are tough, intractable guerrillas who know about fighting in the rugged mountains.

The Kurdish homeland begins near the biblical Mount Ararat in Turkey and extends south to the Persian Gulf in a long chain of mountains parallel to the Tigris River. The estimated 12,000,000 Kurds are today divided among four nations: Turkey, Iran, Syria, and Iraq. Some Kurds also live in Soviet Armenia.

A rugged people of the Islamic faith, they raise flocks of short-legged sheep in the high valleys, where no lowlander in his right mind penetrates without permission.

Leading the rebellious Kurds in Iraq is the *mullah* (religious teacher) Mustafa al-Barzani, a burly, dark-haired, handsome man equally at ease in Soviet Russia and in Paris' Latin Quarter. Just after World War II, Barzani ruled a Soviet-supported Republic of Kurdistan until it was crushed by the Iraqi government in 1946. Barzani remained in Russia until General Abdul Karim el-Kassem staged his successful rebellion against King Faisal and Premier Nuri as-Said in July 1958. Barzani briefly tried to cooperate with Kassem, only to turn against him when it became clear that the new regime was reneging on its promise to create a self-governing Kurdistan. Barzani then fled to Paris, leaving the command of the rebellion in the expert hands of his son Idriss.

Barzani, who has been alternately accused of being pro-Soviet and pro-British, Communist and anti-Communist, has become adept at obtaining support from any available source. His newest source of weapons seems to be neighboring Iran, which serves as a sanctuary for Kurdish infiltrators. A "Voice of the Iraqi People" backing the Kurdish rebellion is broadcasting from, of all places, Communist Bulgaria. Ideology, however, has little appeal for the fiercely independent Kurds, who, so far, have outlived any regime in Baghdad. The rebellion costs the Iraqi government approximately $700,000 a month.

Holed up in their isolated mountains, the Kurds have checkmated four-fifths of the 50,000-man Iraqi army equipped with British jets, Soviet armor, and Czech weapons. The guerrillas call themselves *Pesh Merga,* which means something like "Kurd Freedom Fighters." Being Arabs and natives of the land does not much help the valley-reared Iraqi soldiers. They seem unable to catch the small bands of swift Kurds, who intermittently raid isolated Iraqi outposts and murder local officials. Recently, larger battles pitting Iraqi battalions against well-armed Kurdish units have taken place.

The present strategy of the Iraqi army is to cut off the only road between the Kurdish mountain stronghold and Iran. In 1966 the army fielded 35,000 men against the Kurdish corridor. Two Iraqi battalions were air-dropped but soon were caught in a trap. In the bitterly fought battle of Ruwandiz, the Kurds were said to have captured ten artillery pieces, twelve mortars, and a number of infantry weapons. Reportedly, the Iraqi abandoned 2,000 of their dead on the battlefield. The Kurds were armed mostly with light machine guns and mortars and, for once, did not disappear into the hills when the army attacked.

The Kurds are demanding regional autonomy with a Kurdish legislature and administration, a proportionate share for Kurds of all oil revenues (the rich Mosul and Kirkuk fields are in Kurdistan), special Kurdish army and police units, and, finally, the appointment of a Kurdish vice president in Baghdad. As no Iraqi government seems prepared to accept these demands, the Kurdish question appears destined to remain open for a long time. The Kurds, for that matter, are never tired of fighting—they have been at it since the Greek general Xenophon crossed their homeland on his return from Persia, 400 years before Christ.

THE ARABS VS. THE ISRAELIS: CENTURIES OF CRISIS

The issues in the conflict between Jews and Arabs go back to the 19th century, when Zionist settlers began filtering into Palestine, then part of the Turkish Empire, with the dream of creating a modern Jewish state in their biblical homeland. During World War I, in an effort to win Jewish backing for the war against Germany, the British government issued the Balfour Declaration, pledging support for the Zionist cause. When the war ended, the League of Nations gave Britain the trusteeship over Palestine, but pro-Arab sentiment in Britain and fierce opposition to Zionist settlement in Palestine led the British to renege on their promise. As World War II approached, Jewish immigration into the country was nearly halted, and terrorism between Arab nationalists and Jewish settlers was rampant.

Immigration resumed shortly after World War II when the Jewish Agency, in open defiance of Great Britain, smuggled into Palestine whole shiploads of destitute Jewish survivors of Nazi extermination camps in Europe. At the same time, clandestine Jewish commandos began to harass British officials in Palestine, whom they accused of favoring the Palestinians against the Jews. Arab terrorists, resenting the installation of Jews on Palestine's most arable lands, stepped up their attacks against Jewish settlements organized into self-defense communities. A three-way civil war between Jews, Arabs, and British plunged the country into a reign of terror.

In 1947 the British government turned the problem over to the United Nations, and in November the General Assembly voted to partition Palestine into Jewish and Arab states. The Arabs refused to accept, and vowed to push the Jews into the sea. But on May 14, 1948, David Ben-Gurion defiantly declared Israel's independence. The Arab reaction was immediate: The armies of Egypt, Jordan, Iraq, and Syria and contingents from Saudi Arabia invaded the new state. Outnumbered 20 to 1, Israeli soldiers nevertheless outfought the Arabs who were forced to ask for a cease-fire after eight months of warfare. During the war, 750,000 Palestinian Arabs fled from the land of their ancestors to drab refugee camps in Arab countries, where guerrillas were recruited to fight against Israel.

Although they put down their guns, the Arabs refused to recognize the existence of the State of Israel, and they swore vengeance. The Israelis had won the war, but they nearly lost the peace. In 1949 a U.N.-sponsored agreement gave Jordan control of most of Arab Palestine, except for Jerusalem, which was divided between Israel and Jordan. Egypt kept the populous Gaza Strip, and Syria the strategic Golan Heights commanding Lake Tiberias and riverine Jewish settlements. The agreement left Israel with borders open to infiltration from neighboring Arab states. In May 1950, the United States, Great Britain, and France issued a Tripartite Declaration guaranteeing the integrity of Arab and Israeli borders. But clashes continued intermittently along the long desert frontier.

Tensions alternately rose and subsided during the ensuing years. In Egypt, Gamal Abdel Nasser came to power and began to dream his dream of Arab unity. In 1956, after Nasser nationalized the Suez Canal, Israel joined with Great Britain and France in their effort to regain control of the waterway. The three countries acceded, however, to the establishment of a U.N. force in the area.

The Arab-Israeli crisis deepened in 1966, as Syrian terrorists launched a campaign of sabotage against Israel, and Syria and Egypt signed a defense agreement establishing a joint military command. Syrian-Israeli clashes continued into the spring of 1967, culminating in an air battle in which six Syrian MIG's were destroyed. In May Egypt demanded removal of the U.N. Emergency Force from the Gaza Strip and blockaded the Gulf of Aqaba against Israeli shipping, which Israel termed an act of aggression.

On June 5 full-scale war erupted, and six days later Israel had won an overwhelming victory, occupying 26,100 square miles of Egyptian, Syrian, and Jordanian territory. Egypt's losses totaled 10,000 soldiers and 1,500 officers killed, 5,000 soldiers and 500 officers taken prisoners. Most of her aviation and armored units were destroyed, and Egyptian oil wells in the Sinai—producing three times Israel's needs—were in Jewish hands. The Jordanian army practically ceased to exist, and the Syrians were humiliated despite the military defenses built for them by Soviet technicians. Because of excellent organization and superior planning, the Israelis were able to mobilize 300,000 men, including 150,000 from the reserves; a tank force of 1,000 vehicles, and an air force of 270 jet aircraft and helicopters. It was modern warfare at its most efficient.

Israel's success in surviving against a hostile environment that has challenged the fortitude of the Jews and tested their ability to fight against crushing odds is credited to their sense of inventiveness and organization. Several military and paramilitary organizations played a key role in the formative years of the State of Israel.

The Haganah (defense) created in the early 1900's by Jewish settlers in Palestine provided protection from Bedouin raids against Jewish frontier settlements. The *hashomer* (watchers) were mounted volunteers who patrolled the countryside in the manner of American scouts in the days of the Indian wars.

After the British victory of 1917 against the Turkish occupants of Palestine, the Jews were obliged to surrender their weapons to the British, who became responsible for enforcing law and order. However, during the bloody Arab rioting of 1920-21, British protection proved utterly inadequate as many Jews fell victims of the Bedouins. The British then agreed to distribute a limited number of shotguns to Jewish settlements, but the weapons were locked in special boxes that could be opened only by the *muktar* (village chief) if the village was under immediate danger —frequently after the hit-and-run looters had disappeared in the desert. This clumsy arrangement left the Haganah volunteers with little choice other than to organize their own secret armory with smuggled weapons. In 1929 the British once more stripped the Jewish settlements of weapons. The semilegal Haganah·volunteers, where they existed, took over the protection of Jewish communities.

Shortly thereafter, Arab attacks against the Jews resumed with vicious frequency. When Haganah volunteers were present, the attackers were almost always thrown back; elsewhere, Jewish settlers were often massacred or their homes looted. The Haganah feverishly began to build up its stock of weapons, buying rifles from every possible source

—even from Arabs who had received them from the famed Lawrence of Arabia to fight the Turks.

After 1930, the British permitted the Jews to organize self-defense. They allowed the Haganah to create a small police force in each farm settlement, but forbade pursuit of attackers beyond the limits of the village. A year later, after Arab terrorists had sabotaged the vital oil pipeline from Iraq to the Haifa terminal, the Haganah was given a new importance. Captain Orde Wingate, a brillant specialist in guerrilla warfare, was assigned to Palestine by the British army to organize resistance to Arab terrorists. Wingate, a very unconventional officer—he spoke fluent Hebrew—immediately went to work with the Haganah. He selected volunteers for the Palmach—the military units—and for the famed Special Night Squads (SNS), trained to patrol, scout, lay ambushes, and fight at night. Wingate himself led several raids in Arab-occupied hills to demonstrate the feasibility of night operations in the countryside.

Wingate instructed the volunteers of his SNS to carry their weapons always loaded at night, but to hold fire until the enemy was in contact with the barrel of their rifles. When challenged by an enemy in the dark, they were to answer in his own language to confuse him and make him hesitate. If caught under enemy fire, they were to lie flat on the ground, because the Arabs often misjudged distance when firing in darkness. (At night, it is largely useless to open fire if a target is beyond 300 feet; night fighting is essentially close combat.) Many of the young men trained by Wingate in the Special Night Squads joined the crack Jewish Brigade organized by the British during World War II and eventually became the leaders of the Israeli armed forces.

The Palmach were the Haganah's shock troops, recruited from full-time volunteers to defend the settlements most exposed to Arab harassment. (During World War II, the Palmach supplied some of the daring raiders who operated behind the lines of the German Afrika Korps; these Jews were selected for their ability to speak and look like Germans and their familiarity with the terrain.) Eventually, almost every able-bodied man and woman (except the orthodox) among Palestine's 400,000 Jews were enrolled either in the Haganah or the Palmach. Meanwhile, weapons were constantly obtained in one way or another, often illegally, to create clandestine reserves of arms to be used against both the British and the Arabs.

The Irgun Zvai Leumi (National Military Organization), known as Irgun, was a splinter group that broke away from the Haganah in 1937 to protest the moderation of its leaders. The Irgun was created by Vladimir Jabotinsky, an ebullient Jewish intellectual from Russia. Jabotinsky believed it was necessary to answer Arab terrorism blow for blow and was angered by the pacifism of the older Jews who still relied on the British for protection. The other leader of the Irgun was Abraham Stern, a 30-year-old revolutionary poet who was regarded as a dangerous extremist by the majority of the Jewish community. Organized as a secret society, the Irgun had a membership of about 800 young men living under strict military discipline. If captured by the British, they faced long jail sentences and even torture. Several were hanged.

The Irgun organization included the following groups: *Command Headquarters* comprised five men whose true names were unknown to the rest of the membership. *Personnel* recruited and screened new members. *Planning* laid out plans for reprisal raids against Arabs and attacks on British paymasters and armories. *Training* taught the various tactics of guerrilla warfare. *Supplies* took care of the clandestine arms caches, equipment for printing propaganda, and procurement of uniforms. *Quartermaster services* manufactured explosives, repaired weapons, and provided false identity papers. *Transport,* with the help of friendly cab and truck drivers, provided safe transportation to members of the organization on missions. *Medical Services* maintained a list of Jewish doctors and medical workers willing to treat Irgun members who had been wounded or required medical attention. *Action* was the group involved in raids, bomb throwings, and thefts of weapons and funds for the organization. In fact, the Irgun was the perfect prototype of the secret guerrilla cell. The only slot that might have been added to its table of organization would be a Communication Group in charge of liaison and preparing codes. Secrecy was rigidly imposed and respected. No member of the Irgun was allowed to know the real identity of his officers, and none could participate in the activity of groups other than his own. Jewish nationalism provided the Irgun members—called terrorists by the British—with the will to risk all dangers for their cause.

But even the Irgun was not aggressive enough to satisfy a smaller group of Jews who rallied behind Abraham Stern. Stern hated the British occupiers even more than he did the Arabs. The split between Stern and other Irgun leaders came over the decision on whether to continue the harassment of the British during World War II. Stern opposed any truce with the British.

In June 1940 Stern and some 200 members of the Irgun created their own resistance organization, which became known both as the Stern Group and as the Lehi, Combatants for the Freedom of Israel. The Stern Group was so extremist and so dedicated to violence that many patriotic Jews denounced it as an anarchist movement. Its philosophy was that the cause of Israel's freedom justified every means, even the use of terror. Terror, thought Stern, was the best way to dramatize the Jewish cause and make the situation untenable for the British. Members of the Stern Group were hunted like animals by British counterintelligence in Palestine, and many Jews refused to shelter them even when they were sought by the police.

Stern Group members made several attempts on the lives of British officials in Palestine. No one held a post high enough to put him out of reach of the arm of the terrorists —not even Sir Harold Macmichael, the British High Commissioner in Palestine. On November 6, 1944, two young Stern Group members shot and killed Lord Moyne, the highest-ranking British official in the Middle East, one of the richest men in England, and a close friend of Prime Minister Winston Churchill. Eventually, Abraham Stern was captured and killed in a Tel Aviv apartment by Captain Geoffrey Morton, chief of British counterintelligence in Palestine. But quite a few members of the Stern Group escaped the dragnet to continue their relentless terrorist campaign against British officials and Arabs.

Since Israel's 1967 conquest of Arab-populated territories —the Gaza Strip, Jordan's West Bank—a wave of terrorism has drawn world attention to the activities of several Arab guerrilla organizations. Israel's Muslim population, 261,000 before the June war, has been swollen to 1,200,000 men and women, who retain strong political and religious ties with neighboring Arab countries. Not included among Muslims is the hill-dwelling Druse community, whose obscure religion and mores are little known to outsiders. Druses have joined the Israeli army and fought against Syrian and Jordan troops. Unlike the Arabs, the Druses are regarded by the Jews as loyal citizens of Israel.

Although Arabs living in Israel enjoy complete religious

freedom, they are discriminated against in employment and
are segregated in Arab villages and quarters. Until recently
their settlements were under military government, and
Arabs had to obtain special passes to travel within Israel.
Palestinian Arabs were not regarded as sufficiently reliable
to be accepted in the Israeli armed forces; Israeli police considered them potential fifth columnists and kept a close
watch on their villages to prevent their use by terrorist infiltrators.

Permanent peace along the frontiers of Israel does not
exist, and several Palestinian organizations financially supported by Arab countries are waging guerrilla war to frustrate the Jews of their military victory. The rash of Arab terrorism is directed at roads, railroads, and industrial installations. Land mines are planted in areas patrolled by Israeli
soldiers. The professional jobs are the work of Syrian-trained
terrorists of El Fatah (the conquest) organization. Known
as *fedayin* (soldiers), the terrorists are trained by Syrian and
Algerian instructors in three camps of about 1,000 men each,
built along the frontiers of Israel. The military branch of El
Fatah—responsible for carrying on the guerrilla war—is
known as El Asifa (thunderstorm). Helped and encouraged by several Arab countries, El Fatah is regarded as a dynamic organization opposed to any settlement with Israel.
It has criticized Egypt and Jordan for having agreed to the
U.N.-sponsored cease-fire with Israel.

Five months after the June war, several Arab resistance
movements operating within Israel held a clandestine meeting in Jerusalem. The movements agreed to join forces and
form the Palestine Liberation Organization (POL). As
leader, the POL elected Ahmed Shukairy, a plump, graying,
fire-breathing foe of Israel, who enjoyed Egyptian support.
But in December 1967 Shukairy—accused of talking too

loudly and doing little or nothing—was replaced by Yekia Hammoudah, who advocates a long guerrilla war inside Israel to force the Jews to surrender the territories seized from the Arabs since 1948.

So far, Israel's answer to the guerrillas has been the threat of brutal reprisal against Arab villages. Within Israel there is also strong pressure on the government of Premier Levi Eshkol to permit young Jews to settle 150 farms in the long-occupied Arab territories, mainly in the West Bank of the Jordan River.

In the ten months following the June war, the Israelis killed or captured nearly 2,000 of the El Fatah saboteurs who almost daily harassed the Jews by incidents of mine-laying, bombing, and sniping in the occupied West Bank and in the Beit Shean area of Galilee. It is unlikely, however, that El Fatah squads were able to recruit many active supporters among Arabs living in Israel. Not that they did not try, but the Israelis, aided by good intelligence (many Jews speak fluent Arabic), have always been able to prevent the installation of important guerrilla bases on their territory.

El Fatah's activities are still mainly carried on by commando units of 30 to 40 men, launching hit-and-run raids from Jordan. By the end of 1967 it appeared that King Hussein was losing control of his 70,000-man army and was no longer able to restrain the 20,000 well-trained, well-equipped Palestinian guerrillas using Jordan as a sanctuary for their operations against Israel. The *fedayin*—80 percent of whom never return from their suicide raids—are regarded as heroes in the Arab world.

In February 1968, fearful of Israeli retaliation, Jordan's Interior Minister Hassan al-Kayed condemned the actions of guerrillas against Israel. He said that the government of

King Hussein was "prepared to strike with an iron fist" against activities that "will provide Israel with excuses to mount pressure on Jordan." There was no sign, however, that El Fatah commandos were prepared to desist. Wearing camouflage uniforms and carrying automatic weapons, they continued to move in full view of the Jordanian police. In an indirect warning to King Hussein, El Fatah announced that it will not allow "anyone or any regime" to prevent it from undertaking operations against Israel, "and we will not lay down our arms."

The tension between Israel and Jordan came to a climax on March 21, 1968, in a major retaliation raid. Moving at night, 15,000 Israeli troops spearheaded by tanks and Mirage jet fighters smashed across the cease-fire line, hitting installations of El Fatah saboteurs across the Jordan River. By late afternoon, the Israelis had returned to their bases—minus fifteen dead—claiming to have killed 150 guerrillas. It remained to be seen, however, if Israel's policy of massive retaliation would effectively deter further guerrilla raids or, on the contrary, would only weaken King Hussein's control over the saboteurs. Statements by Israeli Defense Minister Moshe Dayan and Chief of Staff Gen. Haim Bar-Lev gave a clear warning that Israel might take even more drastic action if the incidents continued.

CHAPTER 3

CUBA'S BARBUDOS

"Why does the guerrilla fight? He is a social reformer. He takes up arms in response to widespread popular protest against an oppressor, impetuously hurling himself with all his might against anything that symbolizes the established order."
Che Guevara

On December 2, 1956, a group of eighty-one young men, led by a tall, youthful ex-law student, landed on the coast of Cuba. Although more than half their number were killed or captured in making the landing, the survivors quickly pushed on from their marshy beachhead to the Sierra Maestra, the rugged mountain range dominating Oriente Province on the eastern tip of the island. By any standards they were a weak force, and they drew only derision from Cuban dictator Fulgencio Batista, who ruled the island with an iron fist.

Two years later Havana was cheering the victory of Fidel
Castro and his *barbudos* (in the mountains his men had let
their beards grow, hence the term *barbudos,* bearded ones,
for his soldiers). Batista had fled to the Dominican Republic. The bloody civil war had cost more than 20,000 lives,
seriously damaged the Cuban economy, and set the stage
for the development of a socialist republic only 90 miles
from Key West. What happened?

Perhaps Batista's army, large and well armed, could have
flushed the rebels out of the mountains—no one will ever
know. Instead, the army and police tried increased terror
to prevent the revolutionary movement from spreading or
receiving aid. Result: a flood of recruits and the support of
the Cuban intelligentsia for Castro. One year after his landing, Castro's little guerrilla band had grown to 600 men,
mainly recruited among impoverished local farm people
and to some extent from radical students in Havana.

To disrupt the Batista regime, Castro struck at the sugar
latifundios (large plantations running to thousands of
acres) and also tried to discourage tourism to the island. His
partisans put the torch to *latifundio* cane fields, and bomb
explosions in Havana announced to tourists that the country
was at war. Meanwhile, Castro's irregular army moved from
the hills to the foothills, avoiding decisive battles with
Batista's forces. From the beginning Castro's most ardent
supporters were the dirt-poor farm people and nationalistic members of the middle class. Also from the beginning,
Batista made the mistake of committing his army piece-
meal to the battle instead of attempting to destroy the insurrection in the bud. His troops were not trained to fight
in mountainous terrain, in which the rebels were at
home, hiding in the tangled rain forest and moving constantly. Despite orders from Batista, peasants in the foothills

continued to supply Castro's men with food and "intelligence." Batista's troops patrolled the main roads, but they were reluctant to move into the mountains, and the trails remained in the hands of the guerrillas who moved at night and silently.

At the end of 1957, only two main columns of guerrillas were operating in the Sierra Maestra, with intermittent outside contacts. Fidel led a group of 120 men, and his lieutenant Ernesto "Che" Guevara, another group of 40. In October, Che tried to create a "liberated area" in El Hombrito Valley. With twenty men he built semipermanent installations: an infirmary, an oven to bake bread, some repair shops, and a small press on which the first copies of *El Cubano Libre* were printed. Soon the army reacted and invaded the valley. Too few to defend the base, the Guevara group pulled back toward the mountains where it was rescued by the stronger column led by Fidel Castro. Only in April 1958 were the rebels able to set up a permanent base in the Sierra. Before that, they were constantly on the move and, as one of them said later, "carrying our base on our backs, just like snails."

The main threat to the rebels in the mountains came from spies that the Batista police infiltrated among the peasants. Eutimio Guerra, Castro's first local guide in the Sierra Maestra, received 10,000 pesos from the police to murder him, but Guerra was accidentally unmasked. After that, Castro was cautious with anyone outside his small group of original followers. Let us go back in time.

Fidel Castro was a young lawyer when, in 1953, he commemorated the centennial of Cuba's independence hero, José Martí, with an attack on the Moncada army barracks in Santiago, Oriente Province. The attack failed, Fidel Castro and the survivors of his group were captured and jailed.

The date of the attack on the Moncada was to name a movement—26 *de Julio*—and Fidel Castro's speech before the tribunal that condemned him, given the title *History Will Absolve Me* from its closing line, would be distributed in clandestine channels throughout Cuba giving the movement its first program. Eventually Fidel and those of his followers who had survived Batista's jailers were given amnesty and exiled.

During his Mexican exile Castro recruited a new force, the one that would arrive in Cuba aboard the yacht *Granma*. From the start he received aid from wealthy (and not so wealthy) Cuban liberals in the United States, who helped supply him with both guns and money and also conferred upon his movement the aura of middle-class respectability.

Ernesto "Che" Guevara was 30 when he threw in his lot with Castro. Sporting a black beret and a thin beard, Che became Castro's principal adviser on military affairs. His ideas on armed revolution were generally inspired by Mao Tse-tung's and Ho Chi Minh's theories of people's warfare, although he had undoubtedly picked up some practical knowledge in Guatemala working with the defenders of the Arbenz government and from Alberto Bayo, a Spanish civil war veteran who helped train the 26th of July forces in Mexico. Of rather fragile health, Che used to liken guerrillas to "innumerable gnats which, by biting a giant everywhere and constantly, ultimately exhaust him."

Camilo Cienfuegos, who died shortly after the victory of the Rebel Army in 1959, was a confidant of Fidel in the most difficult moments of the war. He was a born guerrilla leader with a gift for accurately and rapidly analyzing a situation and anticipating future problems. Cienfuegos bore the title of *Comandante* (major, the highest rank given in the Rebel Army since the title of general had too many odious connotations).

Fidel's younger brother, Raul, would become the front-line commander later in the revolution, after the insurgents voted to keep Fidel, their *Comandante-en-Jefe* (commander-in-chief), away from the greatest risks. In contrast with the other leaders, Raul seldom hesitated to use terror against his enemies. He was the perfect angry young man with a pistol.

During the early months of the fighting, the Rebel Army's main military task was ambushing small government patrols for their weapons. By attacking at the weakest point of their much stronger enemy, the *Fidelistas* obtained as much as 85 percent of their arms, the rest being smuggled from Florida and Mexico. As government patrols became larger, the rebels set out mines and booby traps to defend their rural bases. Several punitive thrusts by Batista forces were frustrated by the ring of mines around their strongholds. Batista then sent his air force of B-26 bombers against the rebels. But, as elsewhere in similar situations, bombing proved singularly ineffective against elusive targets. Its chief effect was to terrorize the population and further alienate them from Batista.

As is often the case in guerrilla wars, the main difference between the guerrillas and the *Batistianos* was in their behavior and motivation. The guerrillas were convinced that they would be tortured to death if captured, but they merely disarmed most of their prisoners and set them free after a lecture on the reasons for the rebellion. Only pro-Batista officers were held prisoner or executed. This tactic effectively undermined the morale of Batista's rank and file soldiers, who lost what little motivation they had at the beginning (a great proportion of their number had joined the army simply because they could not find jobs). The army assumed an increasingly defensive posture and too rarely came out of its *cuarteles* (forts or camps) to challenge the guerrillas in the hostile countryside. Lacking a compelling cause, the soldiers were unwilling to risk their lives.

Gradually, despite their small numbers, the guerrillas were able to cut roads and rail lines, isolate the coastal cities, and encircle government installations, which usually surrendered after harassment. The basic unit of the *barbudos* was a forty-man platoon. Fidel Castro had the rank of *Comandante,* as did three other leaders in the field, each responsible for a province, and heading up a column of about 150 men.

The first year of the rebellion ended in stalemate. The rebels made gains in the countryside but failed to win organized support from the urban working class (a difficult task since the legal labor organizations were controlled by *Batistianos*). Batista's army was still strong but could not put down the revolt in the mountains. The second year saw the increasing political isolation of Batista and the increased popular discontent with his regime. In the summer of 1958, Batista launched a 10,000-man offensive against 300 rebels entrenched in the narrow Sierra, which could be easily isolated from the rest of Cuba. Several converging columns failed to close in on Castro's hideout, because the Batista commanders were unwilling to take risks. By August of 1958 the *barbudos* were bold enough to attack trains and snipe at large garrisons.

It was at this point that Castro decided that his Rebel Army was strong enough to split up into several groups. Raul Castro took 40 men to the Sierra de Cristal in northern Oriente Province. Che Guevara went to Las Villas Province with 120 men, and he was soon joined by Camilo Cienfuegos with 90 men. Though the big cities were still safely in Batista's hands, the rebels were fighting in four of Cuba's six provinces, and were expanding their operations in other areas, planting the red-and-black *26 de Julio* flag everywhere.

For Batista the end came rapidly, almost unexpectedly. After the liberation of Oriente Province, Che Guevara launched an offensive against Las Villas, 150 miles from Havana. There he defeated the dispirited army garrison of the provincial capital, Santa Clara; he also captured the armored troop train sent by Batista in a last-ditch attempt to hold the city—the train was derailed and successfully attacked with small arms and "molotov" cocktails. The first major city had come under Rebel Army control. In the last big battle, at Guisa, in November, 200 guerrillas, of whom 100 were green recruits, escaped a 5,000-man offensive backed by tanks and warplanes.

Reinforcements sent by Batista refused to fight. He was finished. On New Year's Eve, General Eulogio Camillo, Commander of the government forces, announced the military decision that Batista must step down. Hours later, Batista and as many of his followers as were able to do so were leaving Havana. On January 2 the first Rebel Army troops, mostly from the Las Villas contingents, entered a cheering Havana. Seven days later Fidel Castro took command in the capital city.

Of course the *26 de Julio* victory did not end the history of guerrilla warfare in Cuba. Dissenters from the Revolutionary Government organized and carried out guerrilla movements in the following years, creating bases in the Sierra del Escombray and planting sometimes hundreds of bombs a day in Havana. These attempts, in spite (or because?) of help from the American CIA, were not very successful. A government truck or building might be destroyed, a *miliciano* or *Fidelista* in the mountains killed, but the Fidel Castro government was not seriously threatened. The culminating effort in this direction was the unsuccessful Bay of Pigs invasion two years after Fidel Castro took power.

Behind the failure of the Bay of Pigs was a series of miscalculations. The greatest of all was the belief that an invasion would trigger a revolution against Castro. In fact, internal opponents of Castro were taken by surprise in two ways—they did not have accurate information on the invasion, and many of them were quietly disarmed by a house-to-house search for illegal arms carried out by the *milicia* following the first bombing raid two days before the invasion. Further, just as if they had worn American uniforms, the invading force was stamped "Made in U.S.A.," and this fact turned most nationalist sentiment within the island towards Fidel Castro. Very simply, the invasion force was too large and well equipped to pass for an indigenous, underground operation.

Although the operation was intended to plant an anti-Castro guerrilla group in Cuba, it was executed like a conventional amphibious assault complete with aerial bombing and paratroopers and tanks to seize the beachhead. Worse, the direction of the operation was totally taken over by CIA officials, and the Free Cuban leaders were left in the dark (doubly so, since they were in the United States, far from the action). Also, there must have been a certain reluctance by the CIA to entrust the overthrow of Castro to a Cuban underground movement that largely escaped CIA control. Preferable, from the CIA's point of view, would have been an invasion force that would owe everything to Washington. In this adventure, the United States learned the danger of working with political exiles who are far from the realities of the guerrilla struggle they pretend to lead.

THE END OF A LEGEND IN BOLIVIA

"The inhabitants of the region are impenetrable as stones. You talk to them, and the glare of their eyes reflects their disbelief."   Che Guevara

Shortly after noon, on a stifling day in October 1967, two columns of Bolivian Rangers—no more than 200 men— spotted a handful of guerrillas in a ravine, deep in the Bolivian forests, seventy-five miles north of the village of Camiri. After a brisk fire-fight, four soldiers and three guerrillas lay dead. Four other guerrillas had been captured in the canyon that had been their lair for several weeks.

One of the prisoners, a lean man with long black hair and a sparse beard, was Ernesto "Che" Guevara, the passionate guerrilla expert and former lieutenant of Fidel Castro. Clad in rumpled green fatigues and sandals, Guevara had been hit by a bullet in one leg, another slug crippled his Garand semiautomatic rifle, and his pistol had no ammunition. Unable to do anything else he surrendered.

Late in 1966 Che's guerrilla group had purchased a farm at Ñancahuazu, in the Siles mountain range 400 miles southeast of Bolivia's largest city, La Paz. They intended to use the farm as a base during the toughening up process and later as a supply depot, but local people, observing the strange goings on, began to suspect that the farm was a secret cocaine factory, and as a result police attention was attracted early, making the farm less useful than it might have been.

In the eleven months that had followed their arrival at Ñancahuazu the guerrillas encountered numerous difficulties—above and beyond the expected difficulties of living on the run and off the land. They did not receive support from Bolivia's radical organizations. The leadership of the Communist Party was unwilling to become involved in the struggle, and the one leader who considered doing so, Mario Monje, would not act unless he held command. This lack of support slowed the process of recruiting Bolivian *guerrilleros*. Throughout its life the guerrilla force had a proportionately high number of foreigners—Cubans and Peruvians—in its ranks.

The guerrillas also found difficulty in establishing relations with the Andean peasants. The peasants, often cut off by language barriers and generally suspicious of white men, apparently adopted an attitude of "wait and see." Che Guevara's group was destroyed before any number of them became convinced that helping the guerrillas would be worth the risks involved.

In April of 1967 another serious blow was dealt the guerrillas. French radical Régis Debray, en route from the guerrillas to his native France where he was to organize support for the group, was captured by the Bolivian armed forces. The army was now certain that Che Guevara led the guerrillas, and this of course brought greater military pressure. From that point on the guerrillas would operate in the midst of constant military efforts to encircle and destroy them—efforts made more effective by their lack of peasant support.

Another crucial factor working against the *guerrilleros* was their small number. Although they were able to inflict comparatively high losses in their encounters with the enemy, the Bolivian army had an unlimited supply of manpower and could "afford" losses. For the guerrillas, every man put out of action through capture, injury, or death brought the group that much closer to extinction. Without official radical support or close ties with the peasants, men were almost impossible to replace. Months before final defeat the guerrillas were separated into two groups. The separation was supposed to be temporary, but the groups were never able to regain contact, and in Che's final battle he had less than two dozen men, some of them wounded, under his command.

The death of Che Guevara, with his extensive experience and symbolic association with modern guerrilla warfare, has been a hard blow to guerrilla hopes throughout Latin America. Whether or not the blow was fatal remains to be seen.

CHAPTER 4

A COMPLEX STRUGGLE
IN AN IMMENSE
AND CROWDED LAND

"The enemy advances, we retreat; the enemy camps, we
harass; the enemy tires, we attack; the enemy retreats, we
pursue."

Mao Tse-tung, "A Single Spark
Can Start a Prairie Fire"

The most important single fact about China—aside from its
vast size—is its population. Now standing at some 700,-
000,000, it numbered 450,000,000 at the time of the civil war,
which means that despite the great human losses brought
by flood, starvation, and warfare, China's population continued to increase at an annual rate of about 12,000,000 to
14,000,000. Since 1946 the population on the mainland has
increased by 250,000,000, covering—among other things—
many times the requirements of the various Chinese armed
forces.

No wonder, then, that guerrilla warfare was conducted
in China on a scale never surpassed since. At the peak of
the war in 1947, the Nationalists had more than 3,700,000
men under arms (perhaps 4,000,000 including men serving
in the private armies of warlords); the Communists claim
to have "defeated" a total of 8,000,000 Kuomintang troops.
(The Kuomintang is the name of the political party headed

by Chiang Kai-shek, and is synonymous with Nationalist.)
Opposing the Nationalists were 1,560,000 Communist regulars and 700,000 guerrillas.

A constant goal of Chinese revolutionaries was to reduce
the strength of the Nationalist armies by combat, attrition,
and defection, while trying to attain parity in numbers with
their adversary. For the Nationalists, the loss of 327,000
prisoners and 200,000 deserters in a single campaign was
neither an infrequent occurrence nor catastrophic. The
Communists, although they suffered heavy casualties, were
more careful in husbanding their men. They left fewer
prisoners or stragglers behind them.

As might be expected, China's size (3,690,000 square
miles) had a profound influence on the strategy adopted by
the contending armies. Much of the great land mass—
rough, mountainous, and nearly roadless—offered an ideal
setting for guerrillas. High plateaus and lofty mountain
ranges comprise two-thirds of China's area. Another fourth
is hills and river basins, where the Communists set up their
bases and "liberated areas" in the early days of the civil war;
by their own figuring, they had fifteen such bases—including one in the rugged hinterland of Hainan Island, in
the Tonkin Gulf. Only a tenth of China, mainly in the
north and in the central region between the Yellow River,
the Yangtze, and the Pearl River delta, is alluvial plain.
These rich, densely populated plains, well endowed with
lines of communications, industries, and commercially active cities, were the great prizes of the war.

At the beginning of the civil war, in 1946, the Nationalists controlled the plains, including the cities. Four years
later, by the end of the war, the last 30,000 Nationalist guerrillas had been pushed back to mountainous Yünnan
whence they tried to make their way to French Indochina
and Burma.

In the north the war was largely conventional, involving big, well-equipped armies. The Russians moved into Manchuria a week before the end of World War II and removed a tremendous amount of industrial equipment. Then the race was on between Nationalists and Communists to disarm the Japanese forces occupying Manchuria.

As the Russians revealed in 1967, it took little more than Mao Tse-tung's "self-reliance policy" to defeat the Nationalists in Manchuria. The Russians admitted that at the end of World War II, they turned over to the Chinese Communists "enough Japanese weapons and ammunition to arm at least 60 divisions. Included were 700,000 rifles, 11,000 light machine guns, 3,000 heavy machine guns, 1,800 howitzers, 2,500 mortars, over 700 tanks, 900 planes, and 800 large ammo depots." According to Radio Moscow, Russia declared war on Japan in the last week of the war to prevent the Nationalist Chinese from accepting the surrender of the Japanese army in Manchuria.

Then the center of the fighting shifted to the great central plain, where deforestation had resulted in considerable erosion and many centuries of cultivation had exhausted the natural fertility of the soil. Historically, this area, stretching from north of Peking to the Yellow River, is regarded as the cradle of Chinese civilization. It is flat and lends itself—when not flooded—to the deployment of large armies and even mechanized units.

As the plain offers few areas in which to hide, Communist guerrillas had to devise a special form of fighting known as "tunnel warfare." In guerrilla-held regions, whole villages were duplicated underground, where the guerrillas could safely store their caches of food and weapons. Whenever a Nationalist column searched a village, all the young men disappeared into tunnels, the entrances to which were cleverly concealed—sometimes under fish ponds. All the

Nationalists could find in the small huts of pounded earth or whitewashed bricks were elderly people, pregnant women, and children. Even the cattle had gone underground. Tunnel warfare had already played a role during the bitter anti-Japanese resistance.

Pushing south, the Communist revolutionary army reached the formidable obstacle of the silt-laden Yangtze River. The Yangtze Basin, studded with rivers and lakes and surrounded by forests of cedar and bamboo, contains the large cities of Nanking and Shanghai. Until 1940, Nanking was the capital of the Kuomintang; before it fell to the Communists, more than 100,000 "revolutionaries" suspected of aiding the partisans of Mao Tse-tung, or of being partisans themselves, were executed. In Shanghai, where the Chinese Communist Party had been founded in 1921, the army would gain a firm industrial and economic base from which to launch a new thrust toward the south.

But first, they developed in the watery basin a new form of guerrilla fighting that they called "lake warfare." Small parties of guerrillas traveling on junks and sampans ambushed Kuomintang waterborne patrols on lakes and rivers crisscrossing the soggy plain. This riverine war was not unlike the fighting that would take place in the flooded area of the Camau Peninsula in South Vietnam, where everything—including artillery—moves by rivercraft. Aquatic weeds and flooded forests give the guerrillas plenty of opportunity for hiding before striking at their objective. Also the swamps and lakes yield a large variety of edible animals, frogs, fish, and shrimps that are a welcome addition to the guerrillas' frugal diet of coarse grain. Lotus roots and water chestnuts growing in swamps are also good to eat. To the guerrillas, the area was known as the "Land of Fish and Rice."

South China, wet and mild, was the scene of the last battle in 1949 between the disjointed divisions left to the Kuomintang and a Red guerrilla army swollen by thousands of Nationalist defectors. After Chen Yi's Communist army crossed the swift Yangtze on large rafts, without firing a shot, the Nationalist government moved to Canton, a large trade center in Kwangtung Province, surrounded by rice fields in the Pearl River delta. Spring floods cut the Communists' lines of communication, forcing them to interrupt their offensive. This brief respite did not help the Nationalists, however; they were too disorganized to consolidate their hold on the last restive cities under their control.

Kwangtung, China's southernmost province, lies 1,600 miles south of Peking as the crow flies. It is made up largely of hills that extend westward across Kwangsi Province to the border with North Vietnam. When remnants of the Nationalist armies tried to resist in the south, they found that a force of more than 60,000 guerrillas already controlled a third of Kwangtung. The conquest of the south was a military promenade, and no significant fighting took place there. Mountainous Yünnan Province, west of Kwangtung, a seemingly impregnable natural fortress peopled by a mosaic of colorful tribes, surrendered with hardly a fight. So did Szechwan, the "Land of Plenty," whose 72,000,000 inhabitants rank it as China's most populous province. Along the coast Fukien Province is hilly and forested. Even in the days of Kuomintang control, western Fukien on the border with Kiangsi contained guerrilla bases. The hills rising abruptly along the sea form a rugged coastline, marked by some 600 offshore islands—among them, Quemoy and Matsu, which are still garrisoned by the Nationalists.

STRATEGY:
THE HORIZONTAL
AND THE VERTICAL

"Rely on the peasants and establish rural base areas."

Lin Piao

In his well-documented book *The Communist Conquest of China* French General Lionel Max Chassin (who had access to intelligence reports sent by the French Second Bureau from China during 1945-49) offers an interesting revelation. The military doctrine of the Communists, says Chassin, was inspired by the "Horizontal Plan" devised by ancient Chinese dynasties. The strategy called for the control of an east-to-west strip of land, which—roughly following the course of the Yellow River—extended from the Red bases at Yenan (Shensi Province) eastward to the Shantung Peninsula. In effect, this prevented the Nationalists from establishing a corridor between their southern stronghold and the economically vital Manchurian plain.

For the reoccupation of Manchuria, Nationalist troops were dependent upon an air- and sea-lift performed by the United States, unable as they were to move their armies overland from Canton to Dairen.

Conversely, Nationalist generals sought to apply the "Vertical Plan," which called for a north-south bulwark confining the enemy to the poorer western provinces and preventing their access to the great eastern plain. The backbone of the "Vertical Plan," as tried by the Nationalists, was the long rail line extending from Canton all the way to Peking and Harbin. In practice, neither side was able to accomplish in totality these two alternate strategies. At the end of World War II, however, base areas controlled by Communist guerrillas by and large followed an east-west axis solidly anchored in the Shansi mountains and thrusting toward the hilly region of Shantung. Corridors controlled by the Nationalists separated the Communist enclaves in a more or less effective way.

In the beginning, situation maps of the Chinese civil war (called the Third Revolutionary Civil War by the Communists) showed concentrations of Communist strength as red spots in remote areas far from the main lines of communication. On a relief map, it was noticeable that the location of these spots often coincided with hilly areas. As the Red guerrillas gained ground, the spots grew in size, but were still separated from each other. Then new spots began to appear south of the Yellow River and even south of the Yangtze.

"White" areas controlled by the Nationalists often followed the outline of the principal rail lines, which were the arteries used by the Kuomintang armies to haul troops and supplies and also served, along with rivers and canals, as the main arteries of trade. This spidery and vulnerable communications network gave shape to the war much more than did the roads, which have never played a role in long-distance communication in China.

The presence of a single pocket of guerrillas astride the Peking-Canton line could seriously endanger the Nationalist armies, which relied on the rails for their logistics. In such cases, the Nationalists were forced to divert several divisions to "mop up" the threatening guerrilla pocket and reopen the railway. Toward the end of the war, several large Nationalist-held areas whose overland communications had been interrupted by the guerrillas had to be supplied by air. This was the first time air transport played a significant role in an anti-guerrilla campaign; the Communists did not possess significant antiaircraft capability.

Strategically, the Nationalists tried to check the spread of Communist power in northern China by gaining firm con-

trol of lines of communications and from there extending
their influence in the countryside. For their part, the Communists conducted a fierce campaign against the single-
track rail lines, which were constantly subject to sabotage
and harassment. To protect bridges, stations, repair shops,
and marshaling yards, Nationalist troops were spread thinly
over long distances.

By 1947, situation maps showed that the red spots had
grown and merged in amoebic fashion to a point at which
white enclaves were limited to narrow fingers extended between Communist "liberated areas." One of these corridors
extending from Tientsin on the coast to Peking, Kalgan,
and Paotow took the shape of the major rail lines serving
that area. A similar situation existed in Manchuria, where
the Nationalists were aided by a dense rail network from
Dairen to Mukden and Changchun—but the steel-mill city
of Harbin had already been absorbed in the scarlet sea en-
gulfing the north of China. A young Communist general
named Lin Piao was already making himself known to the
world.

One year later, Communist power had spread to the
coastal areas south of Shanghai and to a greater extent
around Canton. Even farther south, guerrilla-controlled
pockets, still small in size, were appearing in the rugged
forested mountains along the border with Indochina. Mountainous Hainan had already been half devoured by the Communist tide that nothing, apparently, was able to stop.

To be sure, some of these areas were small bases behind
enemy lines, from which the partisans and guerrillas conducted "sparrow warfare," so called because it was used flex-
ibly by guerrillas operating in groups of three or five,
appearing and disappearing unexpectedly and killing, de-
pleting, and wearing out the enemy by hit-and-run attacks.

In Kwangsi and Yünnan each red spot signaled no more

than the presence of a guerrilla gang that had taken to the hills and secured a group of isolated villages. But it reflected the inescapable fact that the Nationalists were losing their grip on the countryside and that their enemies within already had discounted any possibility of a counteroffensive by Chiang Kai-shek's demoralized armies.

In the later period of the civil war, the Communist army gradually switched its strategy from primary emphasis on guerrilla warfare to mobile warfare involving regiments and even divisions. Eventually, these operations developed into large-scale action mustering several divisions at one time; big cities and fortified positions held by the Nationalists were stormed by frontal attacks. (Five years later in French Indochina, General Vo Nguyen Giap was to make clever use of the tactics perfected by the Chinese.)

It was mainly in the south that the advance of the Communist army was a true "liberation" in the sense that guerrillas descending from the hills had already secured the ground before the arrival of the first regulars of the army. On the island of Hainan, the Nationalist garrison of more than 100,000 men was simultaneously hit by guerrillas from behind and by a fleet of junks landed on the north coast.

What the spots on situation maps reflected was that the Communist takeover was as much a military conquest as the result of an incurable social and political disease in the camp of the Nationalists. With some limitations, the military and political experiences of the Chinese civil war still apply to other parts of Asia.

KOREA: NOT A VIETNAM

By accident of geography and history North and South Korea present some similarities to North and South Vietnam. The northern parts of both divided nations border on

China; both occupy peninsulas shaped like a flattened "S" with long coastlines; and both were under Chinese rule for several centuries. One might add that in Vietnam, as in Korea, U.S. power came into direct confrontation with Chinese Communist power. While the South Koreans have sent some 40,000 soldiers to fight alongside U.S. troops in South Vietnam, North Vietnam is host to a smaller contingent of North Korean military technicians, and perhaps jet pilots. Weapons manufactured in North Korea have been captured by South Korean troops in South Vietnam.

But to draw a close parallel between the experiences of guerrilla warfare in the two Asian countries would be irrelevant. The Korean war (1950-1953) was basically a classical, though limited, war fought for geographical objectives. It was fought on both sides by conventional armies and most of the time consisted of frontal attacks by large masses of men and machines. The enemy could be led to surrender in large numbers and lay down its weapons once the rear of its main units had been cut off. Unlike Vietnam, the enemy could not easily fade away into jungles or swamps to avoid capture or destruction.

When on October 15, 1950, General Douglas MacArthur landed two U.S. divisions at Inchon, the North Korean resistance crumbled. Half of the North Korean forces surrendered because their long supply lines no longer functioned. Obviously, North Korean soldiers were not prepared to scatter in small groups to break through the encirclement, or to disappear into the hills and continue the resistance. A few did find refuge in the rugged Chiri mountains in southwest Korea, where they became guerrillas, but in too small numbers to constitute a major threat.

Later in October 1950, United Nations forces pursued their offensive toward the frigid Yalu River. The two main

American thrusts were under distinct commands, separated by 50 miles of a mountain mass. This tactical situation offered the Chinese command an opportunity to stage a typical guerrilla maneuver on a grand scale. Marching through snow-capped mountains by night, remaining hidden from air surveillance by day, the rugged, frugal Chinese remained largely undetected until late November, when they totaled 200,000. By November 27, elements of six Chinese infantry divisions, well armed and well led, launched flank attacks that forced the U.N. columns to retreat under snowstorms. Elements of the U.S. 10th Corps were forced to withdraw nearly 60 miles southward down mountain trails to the coast, through large groups of Communist infantry that had cut in behind them in guerrilla fashion. Moving on trails following the mountain ridges, the Chinese volunteers, lightly equipped and protected against the bitter cold by their quilted uniforms, were able to overtake the American rear guards encumbered with wounded, vehicles, and artillery pieces. The Chinese offensive was a combination of fluid guerrilla tactics and conventional warfare. The Korean front was finally stabilized in January 1951, south of Seoul. The Chinese had made the best possible tactical use of the bad weather that hampered the U.S. Air Force and of the terrain that was favorable to guerrilla tactics.

Several factors explain why unlike the Vietcong, Korean Communists were unable to develop large-scale guerrilla warfare: 1) With only 37,427 square miles, South Korea is smaller and more densely populated than South Vietnam, lacking ample room for guerrilla operations; 2) Winter temperatures in Korea reach sub-zero, making the countryside more unfriendly to man than tropical Vietnam; 3) Food was scarce and peasants had little surplus with which to support guerrillas, especially in winter; 4) At least in the beginning, Korean Communists followed the Russian model, and perhaps for this reason paid less attention to developing guerrilla units than the Vietnamese, who were under Chinese influence; 5) Unless they had enjoyed the widespread and active support of the majority of the South Korean people, guerrillas would have been "swamped" and eventually destroyed by the sheer number of U.N. troops deployed in the small peninsula; 6) Although the 22,000,-000 South Koreans were largely anti-Communist, the Seoul regime also had an effective police force trained by the Japanese. Finally, North and South Korean Communists disagreed among themselves.

For most of the time since the Korean war ended in 1953, the 151-mile armistice line dividing North and South Korea has been relatively quiescent. But in mid-1966 the situation suddenly changed for the worse. Small armed bands of North Korean infiltrators crossed the 4,000-yard-wide demilitarized zone (DMZ) by night to ambush U.S. and South Korean patrols. In a one-month period, their forays resulted in the deaths of more than eighty South Korean soldiers and a score of Americans; the infiltrators lost at least 145 soldiers and agents killed or captured.

Aside from the border harassment, specially trained guerrillas have been infiltrated into South Korea by sea. While still small in number, they are the vanguard of an expected major guerrilla movement. South Korean security authorities suspect that North Korea is trying to determine whether a Vietnam-style guerrilla war could be waged successfully to "liberate" South Korea. To defeat such a scheme, the United States maintains 50,000 troops in Korea, and nearly half of the 585,000-man South Korean army is deployed along the 38th Parallel.

From captured guerrillas, South Korean officials have

learned that the infiltrators were thoroughly indoctrinated in clandestine operations. Their missions are to test the South Korean defenses, to gather intelligence, and to re-activate guerrilla bases. Some teams, apparently, were ordered to return to North Korea before the bitter winter set in. Some, obviously, stayed behind. On January 21, 1968, a team of thirty-one well-trained North Korean officers infiltrated Seoul in a futile attempt to assassinate President Chung Hee Park.

As far as one can determine, there are two kinds of infiltrators: the military personnel whose mission is to reconnoiter infiltration routes across the 38th Parallel and harass the South Korean defenses, and the political agents who move in quietly into rural areas to carry out subversive activities. The pattern follows the one established by North Vietnam, and it is not impossible that the North Korean infiltrators have received advice from Hanoi.

Once in South Korea, the political infiltrators attempt to recruit agents among peasants for espionage and subversion. Little terror has been used so far, although instances of minor sabotage are becoming more frequent. One slain North Korean guerrilla carried bundles of civilian clothes, false Korean identity cards, rations for 10 days, and $4,000 in U.S. money. The North Korean guerrillas are almost all officers, organized in six- to ten-man teams, heavily armed with grenades and sub-machine guns.

The infiltrators are not confining their activities to political groundwork, which must have started much earlier. In September 1967, a civilian passenger train heading northeast from Seoul was derailed by a mine explosion, injuring several passengers. A week later, another train carrying American military supplies was blasted by an electrically detonated mine; two boxcars were destroyed and six others derailed. The second incident occurred a scant 18 miles north of Seoul, a supposedly "secure" area. There are hints that the North Koreans have every intention of stepping up the rate of infiltration and ambush.

The motives of the Pyongyang government in reviving its guerrillas in South Korea are, apparently, mixed. They see an opportunity to create difficulties for the staunchly pro-American regime of South Korea, although it is doubtful that they are bracing for a major attack. They may try to undermine South Korea's industrialization program by discouraging foreign investments, and thus frustrate Seoul's hope of creating a viable economy. But the primary motive seems to be creation of a sense of insecurity in South Korea as a move to prevent Seoul from sending more combat units to South Vietnam. In effect, the harassment along the DMZ would be a gesture of solidarity with Hanoi.

To meet the new threat, the Seoul government is creating militia units in sensitive localities. The midnight-to-4 A.M. curfew is again enforced in the countryside, and troops have been ordered to provide security for important industrial and governmental facilities. The anti-guerrilla Combat Police units of the Korean war days were reactivated in the summer of 1966.

Since Korea is a peninsula, it might be relatively easy to seal the 151-mile border with the North by an anti-infiltration barrier (though little can be done to prevent infiltrations by sea). The U.S. Army is building a fortified fence in the 18.5-mile sector of the DMZ held by the U.S. 2nd Infantry Division. This fence includes the latest in detection and deterrence devices as well as iron poles and barbed-wire entanglements. At the same time, South Korean units guarding the rest of the DMZ and the mountainous eastern sector are setting up radar beams and searchlights to watch areas most likely to be penetrated by infiltrators. For the administration of President Park, all this is a signal that the Vietnam war might spread into the Korean peninsula, with or without an anti-infiltration fence.

CHAPTER 5

SOUTHEAST ASIA

"Southeast Asia surely matters more than ever. A region which may have held as few as 30,000,000 inhabitants in 1800—and which is carried under the heading of 'peripheral areas' in some textbooks on East Asia—now holds more than 250,000,000 people, more than Latin America and almost as much as the population of Western Europe. The resources of this area are large, and its people—while not yet capable of the kind of dramatic progress we have seen in the northern parts of Asia—have great talent, intelligence, and industry. Its geographical location—while it should not be in the path of great-power collisions—is crucial for trade routes and in other respects."

Such are the words of former Assistant Secretary for Far Eastern Affairs Roger Hilsman describing a region in which he fought with the storied Merrill's Marauders during World War II. Hilsman was seriously wounded by Japanese machine-gun fire while fighting along the old

Burma Road, but recovered to take command of an OSS guerrilla battalion operating behind enemy lines. He knows Southeast Asia well.

Many of the jungle areas that Hilsman visited in 1944-45 as an American fighting man were still echoing some twenty odd years later, with the angry clatter of machine guns and the "whomps" of mortar explosions. For most of the two decades since World War II, the destiny of the peoples of Indochina, Indonesia, Thailand, Burma, Malaysia, and Borneo have been affected by guerrilla warfare. At least twelve significant guerrilla wars, taking the lives of perhaps a million men and women, have erupted in Asia since 1945. Some of these brush-fire conflicts have been stomped out, as in Malaya. Some, as in Indochina, have died down for a few years, only to be rekindled by the seemingly irreconcilable antagonism existing between Chinese political influence and U.S. power. In other areas, like Burma, guerrilla fighting practically never ceases and goes on with varying degrees of virulence through the years.

By the end of 1968, at least seven Southeast Asian countries, including Vietnam, Laos, Thailand, the Philippines, and Indonesia, were again torn apart by insurgencies, this time no longer against the traditional form of Western colonialism, but against political regimes that in the eyes of indigenous revolutionaries have been unable to cope with the challenge brought by relentless demographic pressure, by increased political awareness of the masses, and by Asian nationalism.

What has happened in effect, says writer John Scott, is that during the past two generations war, education, communications, and urbanization have ruptured traditional Asian patterns of restraint and discipline and have rendered Asians dissatisfied and rebellious.

Along with these developments, the village and family have ceased to exist as the limited focus of allegiance of the Asian peasant. Broadening horizons have made him conscious of his nation, and nationalism has become a symbol of freedom and a new order. The masses of peasants expect nationalism to give them freedom from exploitation and tyranny, both foreign and domestic.

THE PHILIPPINES

"The Huks called loudly for honest and efficient government. The landlords they had previously attacked as Japanese puppets were now called exploiters, and the banner of 'agrarian reform' and 'land for the landless' unfurled."

Colonel Napoleon D. Valeriano,
Counterguerilla Operations, the Philippine Experience.

The Philippines (pop. about 38,000,000), having been discovered by Magellan in 1521 and conquered by Spain in 1565, were ceded to the United States on December 10, 1898. The Republic of the Philippines came into existence on July 4, 1946, by agreement with the U.S. government, after almost fifty years of American presence. The task for the Filipinos was to clear the rubble of the war in the Pacific, build an effective democracy, and develop the resources of their 7,000 islands.

The greatest single problem faced by the Philippines since independence has been the Hukbalahap (Huk) insurrection—at one time embracing a large mass of nonpolitical Filipino peasants who were tired of poverty and wanted a new deal. The Huks had fought the Japanese invaders in the underground movement. As guerrilla leaders or followers, they had acquired a good experience in guerrilla operations and won the sympathies of many destitute peasants. Widespread discontent made a potential Huk of every Filipino farmer. At its peak in 1951, this Communist-inspired peasant guerrilla movement numbered some 15,000 adherents and achieved evident success in exploiting the discontent of tenant farmers.

Between 1946 and 1950, the Huks were the law in Central Luzon, the rice granary of the Philippines. They actually envisaged that by 1952 the movement would have an armed strength of 173,000 and a mass base of 2,500,000, at which time they would seize the government. Troops from the Philippine Constabulary—the national police agency—were thrown into the disturbed *barrios* (villages). But their lack of training and of motivation soon began to tell in terms of poor performance: Abuses committed by members of the force undermined the people's respect and confidence in their government. The security offered in rural areas was almost nil, while the toll exacted by dissidents' depredations and police counteractions continued to mount. Farms were abandoned; travel on the highways was perilous.

The founder and leader of the movement was Luis Taruc, a fiery lawyer and radical leader from Central Luzon, known as the Hukbalahap Supremo.

For several months in 1948, Taruc led the government of President Elpidio Quirino to believe that he was willing to negotiate the offer of a general amnesty for the Huks who would lay down their weapons. The negotiations failed. Taruc, who had been elected to the Philippine Congress, collected his congressman's pay and went back to the hills. After that, the government decided upon integration of the ineffective Philippine Constabulary into the armed forces. The strength of the antidissident forces increased to about 30,000 officers and men. But, unpaid for months, the soldiers felt small inclination to hunt down the Huks.

At this point (1950) emerged Ramón Magsaysay, a young Secretary of Defense who was to play a significant role in the anti-Huk campaign. Magsaysay revitalized the military, gave it a sense of mission, fired incapable officers on the spot, and offered good treatment to the Huks who surrendered. At the same time Magsaysay (who had fought the Japanese as leader of a 10,000-man guerrilla army) attacked the roots of discontent that gave the guerrillas so much of their political appeal. In short, he realized that insurgency thrives where discontent, poverty, corruption, ineptitude, abuses, and other social ills exist, and that in order to combat it, the government must make an effort to reform itself, spruce up its image, and offer the people a responsive administration.

Regarding Magsaysay's influence on the army, Colonel Napoleon D. Valeriano says: "Magsaysay issued orders that troops entering towns and *barrios* were to make no threatening display of weapons, adopt no threatening attitude unless there was clear and present danger. He instructed troops entering an inhabited area to conduct themselves as though they were coming among friends." Colonel Valeriano eventually developed counterinsurgency tactics that made his group the most effective anti-Huk force in the Philippines. The intelligence-gathering apparatus—vital in counterguerrilla operations—was dramatically improved.

Intelligence officers were able to track down the Communist Politburo, imprudently located in Manila. One truckload of documents was captured, and sixteen leaders of the Communist Party hierarchy were arrested. A big blow had been struck at the leadership of the Communist Party. Even so, it has never been clear exactly how much influence it exerted on the many small bands of Huks scattered throughout the islands.

When he became president of the Philippines in 1953, the handsome, dynamic Magsaysay pledged his administra-

tion to provide land and a home to every Huk who would
surrender. The national election that Magsaysay won was,
in effect, the psychological shock that convinced the populace an era of change was coming. The back of the Huk
rebellion was already broken.

Magsaysay increased the armed forces to 56,000 men and
fielded twenty-six battalion combat teams. Where before 100
or more guerrillas would be bivouacked, they split up into
wandering groups of twelve to twenty men. Later, they di-
minished into groups of only three to five men. In 1954 the
proud Luis Taruc surrendered to the government.

Three years later, Magsaysay was killed in a plane crash,
leaving his country at peace.

Although decimated and pushed back into the hinterlands, the Huk movement was not completely dead. In
1960, Jesus Lavas tried to revive the movement, promoting
legal forms of political struggle, agitation, and economic
reform. He was captured in 1964.

In 1966 a new flare-up of Huk activities erupted, particularly in four densely populated provinces in Central Luzon.
Less than 50 miles away from Manila, the Huks levy taxes,
run businesses and influence local politics. The political
platform of the movement is nationalism, denunciation of
corruption and inefficiencies in the Philippine's two-party
system, and the uneven distribution of the country's wealth.

Unemployment in the cities provides the Huks with a
ready recruiting ground. Of a total labor force of about 15,-
000,000, some 2,000,000 are wholly unemployed and an additional 3,000,000 underemployed. The Huks have found
friends and supporters among politicians and even in the
police.

The strength of the Huk movement is currently estimated at from 1,000 to 1,500 hard-core members operating
in small bands of 50 to 150 in assigned "regions," with at

least 20,000 additional supporters in the smaller towns and villages of Central Luzon. Luis Taruc has said there are three kinds of Huks today: 1) hard-core Communists, 2) non-Communist "radical reformers" committed to a kind of socialist and nationalist ideology; and 3) "opportunists," who are bandits using the Huk movement as a flag of convenience. The Huks have control in varying degrees of 1,500 square miles and 500,000 people, including mayors of *barrios*. The new Huk leaders are Faustino del Mundo, called Commander Sumulong, and Pedro Taruc, who is Luis' cousin. Both reportedly belong to the category of non-Communist "populists." Huk gangs are well armed with weapons stolen from the huge U.S. airbase at Clark Field or bought with the proceeds of a thriving bar and taxi operation. The government of President Ferdinand E. Marcos has reacted by sending a 3,000-man constabulary force into the Huk areas.

The Huks apparently are working separately from outlawed Communist Party organizations, mainly active in the Mindanao region, where the archipelago comes close to Indonesia. Some 100 members of the Indonesian Communist Party were said to have infiltrated Mindanao after the downfall of President Sukarno in late 1965. Lieutenant General Jesus M. Vargas, Secretary General of the Southeast Asia Treaty Organization (SEATO), at one time estimated the strength of the Filipino Communist Party as a mass organization of 19,000, a party membership of only 700, and an armed strength of 500. It is rumored that rural Huks and the city-based Communist Party of the Philippines are not merging their forces. But the Huks are quickly regaining confidence. When government forces raided a Huk stronghold in Luzon, they seized a plan to train a regular Huk army of more than 20,000 men, with a fully organized command structure. The Huks are definitely back in action.

INDONESIA

"Guerrilla warfare is the war of the weak against the strong."

"Guerrilla warfare cannot by itself bring final victory; it can only weaken the strength of the enemy."

"The principal requirements for guerrilla warfare are: a people who will give assistance, sufficient geographical room, and a war of long duration."

> General Haris Nasution,
> *Fundamentals of Guerrilla
> Warfare.*

The country's 110,000,000 people are concentrated on some of the world's largest islands: Java, larger than England; Sumatra, larger than Italy; Bali, as large as Northern Ireland; Borneo, larger than France; and the Celebes (now called Sulawesi), nearly the size of Rumania. Although the majority of Indonesians are Muslim, there are about 2,000,-000 Buddhists, as many Hindus (in Bali), and nearly 4,000,-000 Christians (mainly in Amboina). There are stone-age animists in West Irian and in Sumatra.

The Republic of Indonesia is the world's largest archipelago (3,000 islands), the fifth-largest country in population, and one of the richest in natural resources. Indonesia is rich in oil (exploited by Caltex and Shell), coal, metals, and precious stones. Its waters teem with fish. Its jungles produce much valuable timber and an abundance of animal life. Its fertile brown-red soil grows rice, rubber, coffee, and tropical fruits. But most of this wealth is still untapped, and the Indonesian economy is heavily in debt ($40,000,000,000 in 1967). Inflation is a way of life.

Tides of nationalism that swept Asia after World War II aroused the Indonesian people to a five-year guerrilla war against one of the most stubborn and proud colonial powers, The Netherlands. In five years, the weak Indonesian guerrilla army, racked by dissension and crippled by chronic indiscipline, shook off 350 years of near-total Dutch rule and installed the world's largest Islamic republic—a great crescent of islands across the Indian Ocean.

Guns crackled in the jungles, terrorist bombs blasted bridges, raiders murdered isolated settlers on their rubber estates. Young officers such as Haris Nasution wrote treatises on guerrilla warfare, lamenting the "immature nature" of their military subordinates who, too soon, concentrated too much of their limited equipment and trained personnel in forming divisions and regiments—neglecting the buildup of a large guerrilla force.

But the political élan and the collective will to free the country were there. No matter how politically astute and militarily capable the Dutch proved themselves, the task of reasserting their full authority over the restless Indonesians was beyond them. In December 1949, The Netherlands recognized Indonesia's independence. How did this come about?

Immediately after the capitulation of Japanese forces in Indonesia in World War II, a seesaw guerrilla war was triggered by the arrival of British troops, who were soon followed by the returning Dutch. The conflict followed a pattern of truce, negotiations, agreement, fighting, and truce again.

Within eighteen months of their return, the Dutch were able to field in Indonesia a modern army of 130,000 men, thirty days away from their supply bases in Europe. But this was far from enough to "pacify" the immense country. The Dutch then did two things: they restricted their occupation to the main towns and control of major lines of communications; and they created sixteen "puppet" states in other parts of the archipelago where local rulers were cooperative. To supplement their own army, the Dutch raised a local force of more than 30,000 men, mainly from Amboina. Then they revived the country economically—tapping Indonesia's vast resources was, after all, their main reason for returning. The prospect of gainful employment in safe areas lured many guerrillas from the jungles. With their navy the Dutch blockaded the regions under control of the republic defiantly proclaimed by nationalist leaders Sukarno and Mohammed Hatta. In some cases, the British—who paved the way for the return of the Dutch—rearmed their Japanese prisoners and led them into battle against the Indonesians.

Like the French in Indochina, the Dutch could not understand the depth of Asian nationalism, partly aroused by the allies' pledge to bring an end to colonialism after the war. The two colonial powers thought the Japanese occupation of their Asian domain had been but an unfortunate accident only interrupting for a few years the course of their mission to plant Western civilization in Asia, a mission they were ready to conclude swiftly and thoroughly. Leaders of the two Western colonial countries were convinced that it was clearly the responsibility of their nations to "educate" the Asians to be loyal citizens, subjects of either France or The Netherlands. There could be no compromise with the self-styled Asian nationalists, whom the Europeans regarded either as artificial creations of the Japanese army, or as dangerous subversives manipulated by a worldwide Communist conspiracy. Many intelligent Frenchmen and Dutchmen earnestly believed that Asians, with the possible exception of the Japanese, were not ready for self-rule, let alone independence. For their own good, Indonesians—like the Vietnamese—were urged to accept a return to the status quo ante, in which the white man was always a notch above his brown brother. Thinking Asians who did not

share this opinion were accused, in the words of a Dutch set-
tler, of being "ingrates who have forgotten everything we
did for them."

Many Asians, of course, thought differently and gave their
support, directly or indirectly, to insurgent movements.
Once the French and Dutch armies in Indochina and Indonesia had capitulated to the Japanese, these Asians had realized that the whites could be defeated; the white man had
lost his former aura of invincibility. The Japanese occupation, though generally resented by other Asians, gave a
number of Javanese, Sumatrans, and Vietnamese their first
chance at positions that formerly had been open only to
Europeans. Resistance groups who had fought on the side
of the allies against the Japanese had realized their strength
and were unwilling to lay down their weapons and return
to a society that held no future for them. Where the colonial
powers failed to achieve their objectives by force of arms,
they often resorted to political deception and trickery—with
the main result of supplying grounds for Asian bitterness
and suspicion toward the West. The harder the colonial
powers opposed Asian nationalists, the further they drove
these elements toward an alliance with the relatively small
Communist-led insurgent groups that had sprung up
throughout Southeast Asia.

The larger islands of Indonesia are admirably suited to
the conduct of guerrilla warfare: they are large and densely
populated (Java, with the same area as Cambodia, contains
ten times more people), and they offer mountains and forests in which to hide. Sumatra, Indonesia's wealthiest island,
is larger than California, and two-thirds of it is composed
of jungles and deltaic swamps. The tropical climate makes
it possible to sleep in the open most of the year. The countryside has many rice paddies as food supply; the rivers and

forests yield fish and game. Even if cities and highways are in the hands of an enemy, villages and footpaths remain the guerrilla's possession. Sailing small boats, guerrillas can hop from one island to another and obtain weapons in exchange for smuggled nutmeg and pepper in Singapore or the Philippines. A certain amount of piracy has always existed, which offers the political guerrilla already developed facilities and clandestine channels.

A truce between the Republic of Indonesia and the Dutch, which was in effect before the end of 1946, was broken by a full-scale attack of Dutch paratroopers and marines in July 1947. Dutch divisions battled their way into Java and Sumatra, proving only that they could seize any city; they could not control the countryside. The United Nations became interested and were able to call a cease-fire in August, drawing lines between the territory the Dutch held and that in the hands of the Republic. But the Dutch paid little attention to this line, and began to organize regional "republics" where they could, building toward the kind of "federal Indonesia" they had in mind. In January 1948 another truce was arranged, based on the so-called Van Mook Line (Hubertus Johannes Van Mook was the high negotiator for the Dutch). This truce, known as the Renville Agreement, allowed the Dutch to remain in areas they already occupied and required the Indonesians to withdraw 35,000 guerrillas from "pockets" within the Dutch-held areas. Actually, it gave two-thirds of Java and one-fifth of Sumatra to the Dutch. In addition, Sukarno and Hatta were obliged to recognize the "federal" states that the Dutch had set up. The Dutch, however, under terms of the Renville Agreement as well as a prior one—the so-called Linggadjati Agreement of 1946—agreed to establish an independent Indonesia at some future time.

To make matters worse, the guerrillas themselves became divided between Communists and Nationalists—a situation that led to a Communist uprising in central Java in mid-September 1948. After two months, the rebellion was finally put down in a blood bath by the Republican forces. One month later the Dutch launched another military operation. In a surprise attack, Dutch paratroopers seized the capital of the Republic, Jogjakarta, capturing Sukarno, Hatta, and every member of the cabinet except a former governor of the Bank of Indonesia named Sjafruddin, who happened to be in Sumatra and continued the fight from there.

More and more Indonesian peasants and intellectuals ceased to support the guerrilla movement. Some remained undecided, some were willing to go into the areas occupied by the Dutch, and some even collaborated with the Dutch, who made propaganda out of Sukarno's "surrender." The general in command of the Dutch operation declared: "The military operation has come to an end; only two or three months are needed to clean up the remnants of the armed bands."

Indonesian Defense Minister Nasution, however, came to these conclusions:

The Darul Islam guerrillas in West Java were gaining ground. They were in a position to stage battles along highways and in cities, and could move with larger forces because their "people base" had become stronger and larger.

Antiguerrilla war is total war. Its political, psychological, and social-economic aspects must be given proper consideration, and long-term solutions must be sought. It would last a long time—not a year or two—and involve constant patrolling. A passive antiguerrilla campaign, doing static sentry duty, would fail. Only an active campaign would succeed.

In a chaotic region the leaders, whether civilian or military, must be in complete charge with complete power. Their first task was to increase the efficiency of the government apparatus. The second was to win back the people and the villages, urging them to take active part in guaranteeing security. The last task was to annihilate the armed bands.

Soon Nasution was given a chance to put these conclusions in practice. In February 1958 a major rebellion broke out in Sumatra and quickly spread to other islands. One of the leaders was Sjafruddin, who had escaped the Dutch in 1948, and had carried out the anticolonial war while Sukarno was held captive. Now he and the other rebels demanded that President Sukarno abandon his partnership with the giant Indonesian Communist Party (PKI), which claimed 6,000,000 votes.

Plainly the rebels—who could muster fourteen battalions —relied on guerrilla warfare to scatter and wear out Sukarno's eighty-five battalions. The rebels also received help from abroad, parachuted by planes based in Singapore and in the Philippines. The planes were British and American. Unmarked B-26 bombers based in the northern Celebes attacked and strafed shipping bound for Indonesian ports. Then one day the Indonesian army shot down one of the B-26's and captured its pilot. He turned out to be a U.S. citizen named Allen Pope, a former employe of the Formosa-based Civil Air Transport. In this way Sukarno acquired evidence that one source of the rebels' help was the Central Intelligence Agency. To prevent Pope's execution by the Indonesian government, the CIA quickly withdrew its support of the rebels. Meanwhile, 200 government paratroopers dropped by sixteen C-47's swiftly recaptured the Sumatran oil fields, and shortly thereafter the United States hastily authorized the sale of military equipment to the Sukarno government.

The speed with which the Indonesian army was able to

carry out these operations surprised all foreign observers. Nasution had created a small but highly effective force always ready for such emergencies. Then, instead of shooting the rebels, government forces sat down for tea and talks, leaving the rebels with little incentive for fighting. The CIA episode gave ample ammunition to Djakarta propagandists for reviving their campaign against a revival of colonialism and for discrediting the rebels as "tools of the West." Politicians in Djakarta, on whom the insurgents had relied to form a new government, or at least to pressure Sukarno into accepting their demands, maintained a noncommittal attitude. The guerrilla movement in the Celebes dissolved into a military stalemate, then fizzled out. Once again Nasution was proved right: Counterguerrilla war must aim at severing the guerrillas from their base within the people, and must therefore emphasize political, psychological, and economic actions. Being an attempt at pacification, counterguerrilla warfare consists largely of constructive efforts; an ordinary war is mainly destructive. Unless the superiority of the counterguerrilla group is demonstrated, the guerrilla ultimately wins. However, cautioned Nasution, do not assume that no military measures are necessary. Every guerrilla movement has a nucleus of men who will always refuse to surrender.

An undeclared and savage duel was fought in Indonesia following the abortive September 30, 1965, Communist coup against the leadership of the Indonesian army. Six top-ranking Indonesian army generals were murdered in the coup, which involved an unlikely combination of Communist cadres, air force generals, and officers of President Sukarno's elite Tjakrabiwara guard. The premature rebellion, presumably masterminded with at least the knowledge of the Indonesian Communist Party's PKI Secretary General Dipa Nusantara Aidit, ended in the ignominious collapse of the

PKI. In the brutal repression that followed, some 90,000
PKI members and sympathizers, including Aidit and most
of the party's senior leadership, were killed.

Today it is difficult to understand how it happened. During
the Sukarno era, the PKI had built itself as a highly disciplined political force, with 1,500,000 card-carrying members
and perhaps as many as 5,000,000 sympathizers in mass organizations. Even the army and Sukarno's presidential
guard had been infiltrated by secret party members in unsuspected positions. Only such elite army units as Kostrad
(Strategic Army Command) and the crack Siliwangi
division based in Bandung escaped infiltration. But when
the coup against the generals was decided, the PKI failed
to mobilize its mass organizations and to launch a general
strike, which would have paralyzed the country. The army
swiftly moved in, arrested thousands of party officers, jailed
50,000 known Communists, and seized caches of small arms
and ammunition reportedly supplied by China. The PKI
made only a feeble attempt to defend its rural bases in
Central Java (the party was heavily centered in urban
areas), and even Aidit was captured and shot. The new government charged that the PKI was receiving financial help
from the Baperki, the mistrusted Indonesians of Chinese
descent who control most of the Indonesian economy and
trade.

Recent scattered outbreaks of small-scale guerrilla fighting in Indonesia have given notice that the PKI is not
totally dead. A forty-member team trying to rebuild PKI
cells in South Sulawesi (Celebes) was arrested with a certain Martinus Girot sent by the Central Committee to
develop the party network. In West Kalimantan (Indonesian Borneo) a group of terrorists attacked the small
Indonesian air force base of Singkawang on July 16, 1967.

Four air force guards were killed, and reinforcements were rushed by helicopter from Pontianak. The Singkawang base served during the *Konfrontasi* (confrontation) against Malaysia to train 1,000 Chinese of the Sarawak People's Guerrilla Forces. Three months later, the Borneo guerrillas killed six Indonesian soldiers on a resupply mission near Sanggau, not far from the Sarawak border. A General Suharjo, former military commander in East Borneo under the Sukarno regime, is reported to be among the insurgents, trying to arrange an alliance between members of a Communist organization (SOBSI) and partisans of the former president. At the same time, Indonesian officials have denounced attempts by former PKI members to infiltrate the pro-Sukarno Partai Nationalis Indonesia (PNI) to prepare a rebellion in central Java. A new Central Committee of the PKI seems to have been recreated somewhere in Java.

The virtual disappearance of the PKI as an organized party is considered, by some observers, a severe setback to Peking, which maintained close relations with Aidit. China has since pledged its "gigantic support to the Indonesian people's revolutionary struggle to overthrow the Suharto-Nasution fascist military regime." An editorial in the official *Peking Review* has described how the new situation in Indonesia should develop: "At present, the main task facing the Communist Party of Indonesia is to regroup its forces, the scattered people's armed forces in particular, to set up revolutionary bases in rural areas, and to develop the agrarian revolution of the armed peasants led by the proletariat."

THE LESSONS OF MALAYA

During the Japanese occupation in World War II, a Malayan People's Anti-Japanese Army (MPAJA) came into being, armed by the British, led by Chinese Communists. When Japan surrendered in 1945, the guerrilla fighters buried their arms and prepared for an uprising, which came in 1948.

With some variations, similar events were taking place in French Indochina, Dutch Indonesia, British Burma, and in the pro-American Philippines. Obviously, many Asians felt the time had come for a new social order. And they felt strongly enough about it to take up arms and fight in the jungle, in the swamps, and in the mountains until vindication or defeat.

Where enlightened governments were wise enough to make the necessary social and political changes, the guerrilla outbreaks were gradually put down. Where, as in Indochina, the established government tried to resist the political mutation, the guerrilla movement gained strength, or became revived years after its obituary had been published. In Malaya, where almost everything worked against the insurgents, it took a 350,000-man British Commonwealth army twelve years to subdue 12,000 guerrillas—more than 90 percent of whom were not Malay but Chinese. The lesson of Malaya is that there is no cheap and easy way to defeat a guerrilla movement once the fire has been smoldering for a long time.

The Malayan insurgency can be divided into three broad phases: the first saw the Malayan Communists so certain of popular support and of victory over the small British police force, that they all took up arms. This period culminated in the dramatic ambush killing of Sir Henry Gurney, the British High Commissioner, on October 6, 1951. The British, despite the buildup of their forces to 25,000 Commonwealth troops, 25,000 Malayan Home Guards, 15,000 Malay army troops, and 50,000 police constabularies, were losing ground to the insurgents. Every rubber plantation in the hinterland had to be defended with troops; every road patrolled; and every village watched, lest its inhabitants provide food and money to the guerrillas.

The second phase, from 1952 to 1954, saw the success of the measures taken by the new High Commissioner, General Gerald Templer. General Templer quickly revitalized the British colonial establishment and ordered such drastic measures as the resettlement of half-a-million Chinese into 500 fenced villages. Guerrillas were isolated and relentlessly tracked into jungles and mangrove swamps. A total of 5,892 terrorists were killed and 1,700 surrendered. A small tribal Strike Force (the Senoi Pra'ak), numbering no more than 300 men, accounted for more terrorists killed during this second phase than all the rest of the security forces put together. This phase ended in 1955 with the abortive peace talks between Tengku Abdul Rahman and the Malayan Communist Party (MCP).

The final period of five years was devoted to the mopping up of the remaining insurgents, at the end of which the last remnants, numbering no more than 600, took refuge in the forests astride the Malaya-Thailand frontier. But the real turning point had come earlier in 1956, as Tengku (Prince) Adbul Rahman, leader of the pro-West Malayan Alliance Party persuaded a reluctant British government to grant Malaya full independence and Commonwealth status—officially recognized on August 31, 1957.

The new Rahman government was able to create an efficient coalition in which Malays, as local Chinese, Indians, and Pakistanis were called, cooperated with the departing British colonial officials. Food control, which had proved a successful weapon to starve the guerrillas in the forests, was tightened; and in 1956 the deputy secretary general of the Malayan Communist Party was tracked down and killed.

The Tengku even went to meet Chin Peng, the well-groomed Chinese leader of the rebellion: if terrorists still holding out in the jungle would lay down their arms, the Tengku would grant them a full pardon. Communists unwilling to give up allegiance to a foreign power would be granted free passage with their families to China. Some 112 terrorists accepted the offer. In October 1958, the Tengku reportedly paid $50,000 for the defection of Hor Lung, the leading Communist terrorist in South Malaya. A dedicated Communist, Hor Lung had obtained his guerrilla training early in World War II at a special British school in Singapore, and he had commanded a successful anti-Japanese force during the Japanese occupation of Malaya. The Tengku paid out $165,000 in these "rewards," a small amount compared with the $85,000,000 that the British had spent in one year fighting the guerrillas. But Chin Peng would not agree to a surrender. He would accept only the transformation of his guerrilla movement into a legal political party. The negotiations broke down. Chin Peng returned to his jungle redoubt, waiting for better days. In 1958, a total of 700 terrorists were killed, captured or surrendered. The Malayan insurgency took nearly 4,500 lives.

In 1968, British Intelligence sources reported that remnants of the CPM (Communist Party of Malaysia) bands were being reformed in the Betong salient in Thailand's Yala Province, just across the Burmese border. The CPM was thought at this time to have a hard-core force of 700 men, trained for guerrilla operations, and a reserve army of 9,000 to 7,000 men and women scattered throughout western Malaysia. Some efforts were made by the CPM to create a broader-based Malay Patriotic Front on the model of similar front organizations existing in Thailand and South Vietnam. But Malaya was still a country at peace.

BORNEO, SARAWAK, AND *KONFRONTASI*

In 1963 President Sukarno of Indonesia launched a costly guerrilla war against Malaya in an effort to influence British opinion against the creation of the Federation of Malaysia, which he decried as a neocolonialist institution. In a campaign he called *Konfrontasi* (Confrontation), and with the slogan "Crush Malaysia," Sukarno moved paratroopers into Kalimantan (Indonesian Borneo) along its 900-mile border with Malaysia's territories on the big island—Sabah (North Borneo) and Sarawak. Some Indonesian guerrillas moved through the steaming tropical forests into Sarawak to stir up trouble. The guerrillas, supported by left-wing Chinese from Sarawak, clashed with patrols of Gurkha troops aided by Iban tribesmen.

Pledged to defend the Federation, the British committed 50,000 Commonwealth troops (including Australians and New Zealanders) to Malaysia. Indonesia's Defense Minister Nasution, an expert on guerrilla warfare, landed small parties of Indonesian raiders across the narrow Strait of Malacca, into Malaya. Although the Indonesian guerrillas accomplished little, they did tie down more than 6,000 British and Malay elite troops in Borneo, at a high cost to the British.

The Indonesian offensive plans could easily have been successful if the population of Sarawak and Sabah had helped the infiltrators. The Indonesians were relying on the fact that the people of Borneo belong to the same Malay stock, speak more or less the same language, and share customs and way of life with the Indonesians. The propaganda mission of the paratroopers dropped into valleys along the coast was to persuade the farmers to provide food and guides and to support the idea of a greater Indonesia.

Borneo is a luxuriant island, and every acre offers hiding places. Superbly trained, the Indonesian guerrillas could survive as long as they could obtain food. But the Iban, the Punan, and the Kelabit tribes were unwilling to share their meager rice stores with the infiltrators. The British were thus able to carry out an effective food-denial campaign, hitting the guerrillas where it hurts the most: in the stomach. Supported by helicopters and parachute drops, British soldiers could outlast the Indonesian infiltrators in the rugged mountains that cover about 80 percent of Borneo, and the swamps and inundated forest that make up another 10 percent.

A number of Commonwealth units beheaded Indonesian scouts reconnoitering the trails at night. At one time, Indonesian raiders threatened Tawau, a sleepy port of Sabah, isolated near the Indonesian border. To rescue Tawau, Australian commandos made the first combat use of the hydrofoil, a small water-skimming boat powered by an aircraft propeller. Hydrofoils proved themselves invaluable for landing small parties of troops in the coastal mangrove swamps where larger boats could not penetrate. These actions confined the Indonesian infiltrators to the foodless jungle; many accepted a Malaysian offer to surrender rather than face starvation. After the overthrow of Sukarno's government in 1967, the Indonesian guerrillas were given a chance to settle either in Sabah or in Sarawak, where life is certainly easier than in the hungry land of Java.

Konfrontasi formally ended in August 1967 (on the tenth anniversary of Malaya's independence), when General Suharto's regime in Jakarta reestablished diplomatic relations with Kuala Lumpur.

During the confrontation with Malaysia, the Indonesian army trained hundreds of local Chinese in guerrilla and terrorist tactics for infiltration into Sabah and Sarawak. Instead, joined by some 600 to 700 Communist members of the Indonesian army, they faded into the jungle and began to build a strong guerrilla base for the resurgent Communist Party of Indonesia (PKI). The PKI accounts, perhaps, for more than 1,000 hard-core guerrillas supported by many thousands of political cadres in villages and towns along the coast.

Kalimantan, or Indonesian Borneo, is twice as big as Nebraska. Largely uncharted, it is inhabited by 4,000,000 native Dyaks, Chinese traders, and Indonesian farmers. To cope with the guerrilla outbreaks, Indonesian authorities sent to Kalimantan General Witono, a short, highly articulate Javanese, an implacable foe of the PKI. In West Borneo, Witono encouraged the Dyaks, the original headhunters of the island, to revive their old custom. The Dyaks, angered by the murder of some of their own men by the guerrillas, declared a blood war on all Chinese—many of them Indonesia-born and totally harmless. At first, only pro-Peking Chinese were to be hunted down. But soon it was open season on all Chinese, even those merchants and traders who had lived side by side with the Dyaks for generations. In one village, an American missionary reported that 300 Chinese men, women, and children had been burned alive. Everywhere it was burn, loot, and kill.

In April 1968, after six months of terror, the Chinese death toll had reached 2,000. Their traditional shops, selling everything from nails to tobacco, were smoldering ruins. Fleeing the massacre, Chinese left the interior and moved into refugee camps along the coast, where they live even now in desperate condition. There is no place for them to go and no hope for them in a country that still calls them "yellow dragons."

Currently, the guerrilla war has 5,800 crack Indonesian troops tied down in Kalimantan, and General Witono is confident that he has the guerrillas on the run. The Indonesian army is cooperating with the Malaysian forces in Sarawak to prevent the guerrillas from using the border area as a sanctuary. Unless the rebellion is joined by a significant number of Indonesian settlers, there seems to be little chance of the PKI's transforming Kalimantan into the strong guerrilla base that Peking envisions.

But even the end of Konfrontasi did not bring peace to Borneo. In March 1968 the report exploded in Manila that a group of Filipino Special Forces had been assigned the mission of infiltrating Sabah, a section of Malaysian Borneo to which the Philippines lays claim. Only 40 miles off North Borneo, the Filipino army had set up a secret camp to train a Special Forces unit recruited among Muslim islanders. Later the camp was moved to Corregidor Island, where the trainees were subjected to severe jungle warfare conditions. Their unit, christened "Jabida," mutinied, and the scheme was exposed.

The Filipino claim to Sabah (pop. 500,000) was based on the fact that this part of North Borneo once belonged to the Sultan of Sulu, who sided with the British when a British fleet attacked and defeated the Spaniards in Manila Bay in the 18th century. Descendants of the Sultan living in the Philippines have sought and obtained the support of influential Filipino politicians eager to invade Sabah.

The Malaysian government lodged a stiff protest and arrested twenty-six armed Filipinos on charges that they were infiltrators. Making things more difficult is the fact that many small tropical islands lying between Borneo and the Philippines' Sulu archipelago have always been a refuge for smugglers and pirates. Also, 25,000 Filipino migrants work in Sabah.

In Kuala Lumpur, Malaysian government officials angrily charged that instead of looking to the future and solving the pressing social and economic woes facing the Philippines, Filipino politicians were making a futile attempt to revive a mythical Sultanate of the South Seas to satisfy their nationalistic pride and divert the attention of their constituents from more realistic problems. "As a new Federation," said one Malaysian official, "we have no past; we are not prisoners of glorious traditions that would force us to look backward instead of forward."

In spite of differences of opinion as to how it should be achieved, officials generally agree that the union of all Malay peoples now living in Indonesia, the Philippines, and Malaysia (Maphilindo) would be a good thing as a counterweight to Chinese demographic and political pressure in Southeast Asia, but that this union should not be achieved by the devious method of guerrilla infiltrations.

GUERRILLAS IN THE MOUNTAINS OF KASHMIR

The disputed land of Kashmir is the size of Minnesota. It falls from the frigid Himalayan foothills to the balmy Vale of Kashmir, where Jawaharlal Nehru's Brahmin family originated. Kashmir boasts such a tranquil beauty that wealthy Indians flock to it to while away the blistering summer of New Delhi, and call it "heaven on earth." In the snow-capped mountains tribesmen keep herds of Kashmir goats, whose fluffy white fleece becomes the cashmere of fancy boutiques.

At the time of partition, in 1947, the princely state of Kashmir was given the choice of joining either Pakistan or India. The fact that 80 percent of Kashmir's 4,500,000 inhabitants were Muslim pointed to unification with Pakistan. But Kashmir's hereditary maharajah was a Hindu, and although he had signed preliminary agreements with Pakistan he hesitated. Angered by his failure to act, Pakistani volunteers moved into Kashmir to establish Pakistan's claim to the land. Panicked by an invasion of tough Pathan Muslim warriors, the maharajah joined India.

There followed a fourteen-month war, in which the better-trained and better-equipped Indian army bruised both the Muslim guerrillas and the Pakistani regulars who had come to help. Some white mercenaries, mainly aircraft pilots, airlifted troops of both sides into Kashmir.

By the time the United Nations succeeded in arranging a cease-fire, in January 1949, India held the richest two-thirds of Kashmir, including the graceful cities of Srinagar and Jammu. Sheik Mohammed Abdullah, an erstwhile friend of Nehru and a proud Muslim nationalist who served as Kashmir's first premier until 1953, openly promoted a local independence movement. Nehru thereupon clapped the "lion of Kashmir" into jail and introduced a series of rigid measures to suppress other nationalist or pro-Pakistan movements. Abdullah was released from jail in January 1958.

Meanwhile, Pakistan backed a "Free Kashmir Movement" whose incursions sparked a small-scale guerrilla war that was to last for the next seventeen years. In typical actions, the Indian army would send columns of turbaned *jawans* (GI's) on punitive expeditions against a village of raiders huddled in the hills. For a purely local expedition, the Indians would field three to five battalions of bearded Sikhs and small, cheerful Gurkhas, some engineers, a medical detail, and a battery of mountain guns carried by mules. Since the rugged terrain prevented the use of vehicles, reliance was placed on pack transport and mountain artillery. Helicopters would have been useful, although their lift capability in the thin mountain air decreases with the altitude. The standard weapons used in this mountain war were the

Bren automatic rifle, the Enfield gun and the 60- and 80-mm. mortars. The Sten sub-machine gun, possibly the simplest weapon ever used by a modern army, played a role in closer fighting.

With the battalions, gunners, and pack transport marching in long columns on winding trails open to ambushes, it was vital to place sentries along the route, far enough back to keep the enemy marksmen out of range of the main detachment. As the British officer Reginald Hargreaves had noted years earlier, "Few things are more demoralizing for regular troops than consistent, accurate sniping to which it is almost impossible to return effective fire." And the Pathan guerrillas are crack shots.

While the Indians chased Muslim guerrillas, the Chinese army quietly moved into the remote Ladakh area of Kashmir, an arid plateau with a range of peaks rising to 18,000 feet. The Indians had paid so little attention to the forlorn area that the Chinese were able to build a military road between their provinces of Sinkiang and Tibet that cut 112 miles across Ladakh—so the Indians claimed two years later when they finally uncovered the road. By the fall of 1962, an undeclared war existed between India and China, which resulted in severe setbacks for the 500,000-man Indian army. The outgunned Indians had to patrol 2,500 miles of uneasy border with China while suppressing guerrilla movements in tropical Assam and in frostbitten Kashmir, at opposite ends of the country.

Three years later, on the night of August 5, 1965, several thousand Pakistani and Kashmiri "freedom fighters" crossed the U.N. cease-fire line in Kashmir and headed for Srinagar with the intention of instigating a rebellion against India among the Muslim population. To cut off the guerrillas' supplies, the Indian army promptly drove across the cease-fire line, occupying two Pakistani outposts and the strategic Haji Pir Pass. In retaliation, Pakistani tanks crossed the Indian border near the city of Jammu, where they were opposed by Indian jet fighters and bombers.

In a matter of hours the quiet guerrilla war of Kashmir escalated into full-scale fighting involving tank battles, parachute landings, and naval attacks. It was evidently more than the weak economies of both India and Pakistan could sustain for long without massive transfusions of foreign military assistance. As neither side could obtain this, the fighting quickly died down. Ultimately, the threat of Chinese intervention along the Himalayas prompted India and Pakistan to agree to the U.N.-ordered cease-fire. By October 1965 the Kashmir quarrel had returned to the *status quo ante*. Neither side has since shown any serious willingness to resume fighting.

CHAPTER 6

A NINE-YEAR
CAMPAIGN IN INDOCHINA

"Those who have rifles will use their rifles; those who have
swords will use their swords; those who have no swords will
use spades, hoes, or sticks. Everyone must endeavor to oppose the colonialists and save his country."

President Ho Chi Minh
December 20, 1946.

On a damp, uncomfortable day of December 1944, an in-
congruous scene was taking place in a desolate mountain
valley of Tuyenquang Province, a virtually inaccessible corner of French Indochina. A Vietnamese teacher of law and
economics in rumpled business suit and *casque colonial*
(pith helmet) was reviewing a detachment of thirty-four
Tho tribesmen sporting a motley assortment of old French
weapons. The name of the teacher was Vo Nguyen Giap.

A graduate of Chinese Communist military schools, Giap
was a faithful disciple of the old revolutionary Ho Chi

137

Minh, who had devoted his eventful life to denouncing French colonial methods in Indochina. Giap introduced his tough-looking men to Ho, calling them the first "Vietnam Propaganda Unit for National Liberation." In his address to the guerrillas, the gaunt Ho offered a bit of advice. "Concerning tactics," he said, "we will apply guerrilla warfare, which consists in being secret, rapid, active, now in the east, now in the west; arriving unexpectedly and leaving unnoticed." Ho concluded by expressing the hope that "though the size of the first unit for national liberation is small," other units would soon follow.

December 22, 1944 is celebrated to this day as the official birthday of the North Vietnamese Armed Forces (NVA). Who among the self-confident French colonial administrators then in Hanoi could have predicted that ten years later the elite of the French army would surrender to the unimpressive Vietnamese school teacher-turned-commander-in-chief of a highly motivated guerrilla force of 350,000 men?

In December 1944, the French were the only Western colonial power to have maintained a grip on an Asian empire. Larger than metropolitan France itself, the territory had a population of 30,000,000 subjects. In eighty years, hardworking French *colons* had bound a cluster of territories separated by barriers of language, race, and geography into a cohesive political and economic unit.

But Asia was in political ferment, and the French had failed to notice it. In July 1945, Vo Nguyen Giap's guerrilla units in the provinces of Caobang, Baccan, and Langson had grown enough to attract the attention of American OSS operatives based in Chungking, in southern China. The OSS men were eager to develop indigenous resistance movements against the Japanese armies then occupying Southeast Asia. Vo Nguyen Giap seemed to be the man who could do the job in Indochina. A small team of American *gung ho* instructors was parachuted into Ho Chi Minh's jungle headquarters in North Vietnam. To a grateful Ho, the OSS agents offered precious packs of cigarettes. Giap got Tommy guns and grenades for his fledging anti-Japanese guerrilla operation. Giap, who already had an excellent intelligence network throughout North Vietnam, trained and expanded his forces, forming small regular units to assist his guerrillas.

Then a rapid succession of events shook Indochina. The French were disarmed by the Japanese; the Japanese surrendered to the Allies; Ho Chi Minh boldly proclaimed the independence of Vietnam. Then, a 200,000-man Chinese army descended on North Vietnam, pillaging and looting, under the pretext of disarming the Japanese. The ragtag Chinese who had come down from Yünnan soon made Ho Chi Minh regret the loss of the French presence. Ho allowed the French to return to North Vietnam—which they did under a driving monsoon rain—in exchange for their recognition of the Democratic Republic of Vietnam (RDVN). The French invited Ho to discuss things in Paris; he accepted, but continued to exert military pressure on the Vietnamese guerrillas. Nevertheless, the French managed to get the unwanted Chinese out of Indochina (a U.S. fleet transported them to Manchuria, where they defected to the Communists).

It was then that I arrived in Indochina, where the course of events was taking an intriguing twist. The French were divided between advocates of an accord with Ho Chi Minh as a sovereign chief of state and those who simply wanted to assert the *présence française* in Indochina. An atmosphere of despair reigned over Saigon. In the port, stocks of raw rubber were in flames, set afire by the Vietminh (as the partisans of Ho Chi Minh were called). Grenades exploded in

markets by day and in the shabby cafés at night. Cheap
opium was easier to buy than medicine for the thousands
of disease-ridden Vietnamese in the streets. On both sides,
torture and atrocities were everyday occurrences. Roads
around Saigon were unsafe; bridges were destroyed. In
Cochin China (then the name for the South Vietnamese
Mekong delta) the guerrillas were weak; but so were the
French, who had considerable difficulties in transporting
troops and matériel from France. French soldiers were ra-
tioned to twelve cartridges and two grenades; the Vietminh
used machetes and homemade grenades, which, more often than not, were extremely unreliable.

French troops, ill equipped and poorly fed, were decimated by skin infections, dysentery, malaria. Army hospi-
tals were crowded. Men died of unknown fevers or went
mad, tried to shoot themselves, or sold their rifles to the
guerrillas for a few drinks of cheap rice wine. Reduced to a
diet of rice without vegetables or meat, guerrillas in the
forests were stricken by the dread beriberi.

But the French had some good battalions trained during
World War II, and they were not to admit defeat readily,
such was their burning ambition to reassert themselves as a
colonial power. French officials sought to trick the Vietnamese into negotiating while the French army gradually
beefed up its forces in Indochina. In Cochin China, the
French were able to reoccupy the main towns. They sent
troops into Cambodia and Laos with little opposition—
mainly because many Cambodians and Laotians thought
that a French presence was a necessary evil to protect them
from the land-grabbing of the Vietnamese and the expan-
sionism of the Thais.

In the streets of Saigon, Japanese soldiers waiting for re-
patriation looked at all this with amused detachment. A few

die-hard Japanese went over to the Vietminh and fought against the French.

Things were different in North Vietnam, where a brigade of French troops faced some 60,000 Vietminh, 35,000 of whom were regulars armed with weapons "bartered" from the Chinese.

The showdown took place in Hanoi on December 19, 1946, at 8 p.m. Jean Sainteny, the French political representative who had almost won Ho Chi Minh's friendship and confidence, was wounded in the first hours of the vicious street fighting between French tanks and Vietminh troops manning roadblocks. But the guerrillas were no match for the battle-tested French troops who, supported by tanks, cleared the city, reopened their communications with the port of Haiphong, and pushed the Vietminh back to the rice paddies. Before fleeing the city, Ho Chi Minh made an appeal to his countrymen:

"Compatriots, the resistance war will be long and fraught with sufferings. Whatever sacrifices we have to make and however long the resistance war will last, we are determined to fight to the end, until Vietnam is completely independent and unified. We are 20,000,000 against 100,000 colonialists. Our victory is firmly guaranteed." Then Ho vanished into the jungle of Vietbac, the stronghold of his revolutionary movement.

What followed for eight incredible years has become a classic example of protracted guerrilla warfare. To oppose Ho, France sent her best professional soldiers, men for whom fighting in the swamps and the jungle against a crafty and cunning enemy had become a consuming passion. Many of these men, like the paratroopers of Colonel Bigeard, were not satisfied by a twenty-six-month tour of duty in Vietnam. As soon as their six-month leave in France was over, they revolunteered for Vietnam, Laos, or Cambodia. They were anxious to learn the secrets of guerrilla warfare. As it turned out, Vo Nguyen Giap was a good teacher.

By late 1951, there were about 51,000 French troops in Indochina, hardly enough to control thirty or forty main cities and keep roads open between them over a distance of 1,000 miles. Ground troops included the 9th Colonial Infantry Division (DIC), an armored brigade known as the Colonne Massu—from the name of its commander—several units of marine commandos, experienced paratroopers, and the white-kepied 2nd Foreign Infantry Regiment (2ème REI), mainly recruited among German prisoners from the Afrika Korps. There were also Italians, Spanish, and even a few American Army deserters. No task was too difficult for the spirited Legionnaires. Their somber motto painted on the walls of their beleaguered outposts in Central Vietnam was: "Legionnaires, you are here to die, and you will be sent where death is." In Cambodia, and among the tribal groups, the French recruited heavily for their undermanned artillery and infantry units. Later, the *Corps Expéditionnaire* grew to 100,000 men with the arrival of Algerian, Moroccan, and Tunisian battalions from North Africa and some Senegalese units.

But the effectiveness of these African troops was a great disappointment: Most were reluctant to fight at night in a jungle environment quite different from the sandy wastes of North Africa. Better trained for long-range patrols in the Sahara Desert than for knee-deep slogging in Asian swamps, quite a few African soldiers—who could not swim—simply drowned. French-officered Cambodian battalions were among the best, Tunisian *tirailleurs* (light infantrymen) among the worst. As air support, the French could muster only two dozen Spitfires of World War II vintage and a handful of British Mosquito light bombers, which crashed one after another. The French navy was proudly represented by the battleship *Richelieu* and a wide assortment of small amphibious craft. This colorful army was commanded by an ascetic-looking French nobleman named General Philippe Leclerc de Hautecloque, one of the first French officers to have rallied to General Charles de Gaulle's Free French forces in World War II.

The French strategy was to expand their control from the cities into the hinterlands, following the well-tested "oil-spots" tactic. In the flat, humid Mekong delta, roads were kept open during daylight thanks to a series of watchtowers built within sight of each other. No more than five soldiers were placed in each tower, sometimes one or two Frenchmen with locally recruited partisans of questionable loyalty. Whenever they could, the French entered into alliances with local warlords and leaders of various religious sects. This was especially true in South Vietnam, where the Binh Xuyen river pirates, the Cao Dai sect, and half a dozen picturesque Hoa Hao warlords fought alongside the French against the Vietminh. Once a local chieftain had entered into an alliance with the French, the policy was to let him "pacify" one or two provinces—with France supplying money and weapons to his private army. In some areas, this political expediency worked well. Almost single-handed, a wiry Eurasian named Jean Leroy within three years was able to pacify the rich Kien Hoa Province with 600,000 inhabitants. (Today, Jean Leroy lives in exile in Paris, and Kien Hoa is two-thirds under Vietcong control.) The alliance between the sects and the French created many difficulties for the Vietminh in Cochin China and allowed General Leclerc to shift French battalions from the Mekong delta for duty in Annam and Tonkin (Vietnam north of the delta).

Politically, the French could have done one of two things: recognize Ho Chi Minh's RDVN as an independent state within the French Union, or blackball Ho on the ground of his Communist past and negotiate honestly with Vietnamese nationalists willing to join a commonwealth in which Vietnam's economic and cultural ties with France would have been preserved. The French, eventually, chose to deal with the former Emperor Bao Dai, who seemed to despise himself for having to compromise with the colonial power. Bao Dai had little support among the Vietnamese nationalists, who had lost their enthusiasm for an imperial restoration. As they expanded their control over an area, the French reinstalled an administration staffed by pro-French village and district chiefs. But throughout the war, the greatest difficulty faced by the French was to make the Vietnamese administrative machine operate efficiently. In some areas it did, but in Tonkin (northern Vietnam) the situation was quite different.

Vo Nguyen Giap had retreated into the craggy limestone hills of Vietbac, the mountainous region of northern Vietnam, with his best troops—leaving a screen of guerrillas around Hanoi to harass the French. On February 6, 1947, Ho Chi Minh urged his countrymen to carry out "widespread destruction" to prevent the French from using provincial cities and economic installations as springboards for their military operations. Said Ho, "A pick stroke in the road has the value of a bullet shot at the enemy." Answering Ho's appeal, hundreds of thousands of North Vietnamese destroyed their own homes and dispersed the stones and bricks in the forests. When French armored columns reoccupied provincial capitals such as Phuly, Ninhbinh, or Thaibinh, they found ghost towns, completely leveled. In Phutho, the only evidence left of the city was the outline of a sidewalk. This scorched-earth policy, though it was extremely hard on the Vietnamese urban residents—villagers were not affected—spoiled the French initial military success. In a matter of months jungle growth erased the once-beautiful French roads.

Vo Nguyen Giap was trading ground for time to build up and reorganize his forces. I remember a Vietminh slogan left on the wall of a burned-down administrative building: "French soldiers! to your tanks and gunboats we will oppose time and space." In the winter of 1947, the French threw 10,000 seasoned men in a large-scale offensive against the Vietbac in the hope of destroying the stronghold of the Vietminh rebellion and getting rid of its leaders once and for all. Actually, the French nearly succeeded. Their "hit-fast-and-hard" tactic caught the Vietminh leaders by surprise.

Throughout 1948, Vo Nguyen Giap remained on the defensive. With a series of mop-up operations, the French regained control of the Red River delta, winning the "neutrality" of the important Catholic bishoprics of Phatdiem and Buichu. In Cochin China, the Vietminh waged a war of ambushes against French military and commercial convoys, but could not prevent the French from consolidating their hold.

In 1949, Mao Tse-tung entered Peking. In Indochina, the French were suddenly faced with the alarming prospect of a common border with a powerful Communist state lending assistance to the Vietminh. The Chinese Red Army victory was a great encouragement to Vo Nguyen Giap, a student of Mao's "people's war" strategy, and the French government sensed it. In May, General Revers, Chief of the French General Staff, after inspecting Indochina, drew up a plan emphasizing the strategic importance of North Vietnam.

He recommended that the French make an attempt to close the China-Vietnam border to isolate the Vietminh; expand their hold in the densely populated Red River delta; and regroup their scattered battalions into stronger *groupes mobiles* (mobile units similar to a U.S. regimental combat team). Mysteriously, a copy of the top-secret Revers Plan reached Vo Nguyen Giap in his jungle lair: The Vietminh guerrillas were not without friends in Paris. The new escalation brought about by Revers increased to 150,000 the number of French troops in Indochina.

Meanwhile, Vo Nguyen Giap's strategy was to gain time and wear out the French until the arrival of Chinese Communist forces on the border. Giap's intermediate plan was to send out a large number of company-size units to operate independently to the rear of the French, and to combine fighting with political work among the peasants, who were promised ownership of their land if they supported the revolution. Each company of 100 to 200 regulars was given the task of recruiting and training local partisans who would stay in their villages. More guerrilla bases were constantly activated deep behind the French main line of defense along the periphery of the Red River delta, a triangle of 100 miles on each side. The presence of these elusive guerrillas constantly disrupting the French pacification efforts was the nightmare of every French commander in North Vietnam. With his remaining main forces, Giap created "concentrated battalions" capable of challenging the weakest parts of the French deployment. Each campaign involved from three to nine battalions, and gradually the Vietminh acquired enough experience to move into mobile warfare.

As Giap was to say later, "1950 marked a great change in the war." The French had considerably extended the areas under their occupation; they had forces strung along most of the Chinese border, and their presence was felt almost everywhere on the Indochinese peninsula, from Saigon to the Yünnan border. Yet French forces were dangerously thin everywhere, with so many battalions committed to garrison duty that the French Expeditionary Corps was acquiring a defensive mentality; Leclerc had long since left Indochina, replaced by Carpentier, an old-school general with little élan. When in October Giap decided to strike at a string of French outposts along *Route Coloniale No. 4,* Carpentier was caught by surprise and panicked. In a short time, Giap guerrillas routed the French garrisons stationed on the border with China. Retreating French columns encumbered with vehicles were cut off and hacked to pieces. Even the fortress of Langson was abandoned without a fight by its Foreign Legion garrison. As Carpentier was unable to mount a worthwhile counteroffensive, a wave of panic struck the French in North Vietnam.

The incredible fact is that Giap had managed, with Chinese Communist assistance, to transform his motley guerrillas into five *su doan* (divisions) well officered and backed by a complex logistics system relying on long columns of porters to deliver rice and ammunition to the front. Giap's soldiers were thoroughly indoctrinated by political commissars aping the Chinese system of self-criticism and denunciation. Giap had clearly understood the basic principle of "people's war": that politics should remain in command. Political *can bos* were responsible for troop morale, indoctrination, and morality, and they exerted control over the military leadership. The *can bos* also handled the always difficult relations between soldiers and peasants. The peasants, of course, were asked to contribute everything to the war effort. It was at that time that the Vietminh transformed itself into a Communist "people's army." This fact was resented by many Vietnamese intellectuals, who could not suffer the presence of the ubiquitous political commissars. Hundreds of Vietnamese nationalists left the resistance areas for the French-occupied cities.

The guerrilla army that Giap had patiently built had three levels. At the apex were 125,000 disciplined regulars organized in autonomous regiments and divisions. They were well armed, well trained, and could challenge French fortified positions if the ratio of two regiments against one French battalion was observed. The regulars could be moved from one part of North Vietnam to another, or even to Laos. The second level consisted of regional forces; usually one regional battalion per province, one regional company per district. They could mount attacks on smaller French outposts and frighten the Vietnamese partisans armed by the French to protect their administration in the countryside. Whenever the French attacked in strength, the regional troops quickly scattered, only to regroup after French soldiers had left. At the third level were the *du kich* (guerrillas), either one squad or one platoon in each hamlet and village, armed with homemade grenades, booby traps, and various assortments of captured weapons. In the densely populated Red River delta, the pugnacious, crafty little guerrillas, wearing the brown homespun cloth of ordinary peasants, caused many problems for the French.

I remember a search-and-destroy operation in Thaibinh Province where 60 percent of the casualties suffered by the French were inflicted by crude booby traps set up by the rarely seen guerrillas. For several weeks, four French *groupes mobiles*, supported by tanks and batteries of artillery, swept the soggy countryside without coming face to face with the enemy. Almost invariably, when French troops reached a village, they found it empty. But sometimes a Vietminh regional company cornered in a hamlet offered determined resistance. The North Vietnamese villages, protected by thick rows of cactus, moats, hedgerows, and bamboo thickets were natural fortresses in which the Vietminh dug galleries and firing emplacements almost immune to French artillery. The war in the Red River delta was a truly dirty war. The French retaliated against the fortified villages with napalm bombardments and merciless search-and-destroy operations. Despite the disaster suffered on the China border, the French were not yet ready to give up. General Jean de Lattre de Tassigny, the French MacArthur, was sent to Indochina with full power, to redress the situation. De Lattre's flamboyant presence revitalized the dispirited French army. More *groupes mobiles* were created, each one led by the best combat officer France could produce. The Vietnamese army was considerably expanded. Ranger battalions and companies, recruited among Vietminh war prisoners and defectors, were entrusted to aggressive French noncommissioned officers, who wielded more influence at General de Lattre's headquarters than most senior colonels. The Vietnamese serving with these commandos were fiercely loyal to the French warrant officer who led them. The dangerous mission of the commandos, organized much like the U.S. Special Forces A Teams later in Vietnam, was to operate in the rear of the Vietminh and snatch prisoners. Their uniforms were the black pajamas worn by Vietnamese peasants. Before the Vietminh found ways to counter them, usually by infiltration and penetration, the commando teams achieved results. De Lattre had realized that counterguerrilla war is a young man's war, and he was ready to give many responsibilities to those who had proved themselves. Any French officer who did not perform superbly in action was ruthlessly relieved of his command by de Lattre and shipped back to garrison duty in France, very much as Giap purged his own officers. An important point is that de Lattre understood that

North Vietnam was the main battlefield and that the war was going to be decided there. His best troops were mustered in the North. To solve his manpower problem in other parts of Indochina, de Lattre decreed that every French battalion recruit one or two companies of Vietnamese volunteers. This integration of French and Vietnamese soldiers gave excellent results on the battlefield. Vietminh prisoners, known as *pims,* were attached as porters to French battalions, very much as Giap himself was doing.

Giap was flattered by the appointment of the prestigious de Lattre as his chief opponent and was anxious to test him. Giap's master plan was to break through French defenses on the periphery of the delta and then capture Hanoi before the French could react. But de Lattre moved swiftly, smashing a series of three Vietminh offensives against the Red River delta. The French were now receiving military assistance in the form of equipment from the United States, and it made a great difference. The obsolete Spitfires and Junkers were being replaced by American Bearcats, Hellcats, and B-26 attack bombers. Eighty percent of the war's financial cost was supported by the United States.

But adversity was to strike the proud de Lattre. In the summer of 1951, his only son, a first lieutenant in Vietnam, was killed during a Vietminh offensive in the delta. De Lattre was seriously affected and began to doubt his mission. It took him several weeks to recover from his son's untimely death. He bitterly accused his allies, the Vietnamese bishops in Phatdiem, of having betrayed him since they had failed to report the movements of three Vietminh divisions toward their area. Fast, accurate intelligence is vital in counterguerrilla operations and, for once, the intelligence-gathering community had failed de Lattre. Giap had been able to move his divisions in perfect secrecy.

The next move was de Lattre's. On November 14, 1951, French paratroopers landed in the valley of Hoabinh, a major Vietminh communications center in the Black River valley, 45 miles west of Hanoi. But Hoabinh, though a military success executed by 20,000 of the best French troops, was, in the words of a French officer, "like striking at water with a sword." At General de Lattre's invitation, a small group of war correspondents whom I had joined walked on jungle trails to Hoabinh. The enemy was nowhere to be seen. Hoabinh eventually offered Giap an occasion to infiltrate more regulars into the delta, where they created a serious threat to the French.

At that time, de Lattre, who had never completely recovered from the loss of his son, went to Paris for surgery. In January 1952 he died of cancer.

In February, the cautious General Raoul Salan, who had taken over from de Lattre, decided to pull out of the Hoabinh trap. It was a difficult operation through the mountains, but the Foreign Legion fought well to protect the French rear guard. This time it was Giap who was taken by surprise and was unable to react fast enough to disrupt the French withdrawal.

Major military offensives in North Vietnam invariably took place in the fall-winter season; the weather is then dry, and the peasants, no longer tied down by the rice harvest, can be drafted as coolie labor. In October 1952, Giap was not yet ready for another round with the *groupes mobiles* poised in the delta. Instead, he chose to strike in a totally different direction: at French garrisons isolated in the vast and mountainous northwest country. It was mobile warfare again, but this time against relatively weak positions that the French could supply only by airlift when weather permitted. Giap carried out deep thrusts into the mountains, annihilated a

French post at Nhialo, and withdrew quickly before the French could react with paratroopers. Initiative, mobility, and flexibility became the guidelines of the Vietminh division commanders. On the French side, barbed wire, sandbags, and fortifications were the visual evidence of a Maginot line mentality, a poor substitute for aggressive patrolling and alertness. (The Maginot Line, named after André Maginot—a former French Minister of War—was a line of defensive fortifications built by France (1930-34) to protect her eastern border.) From these days in Hanoi, I learned that the amount of barbed wire used by an army is a good indication of its lack of fighting spirit. At that time General Giap was anxious to move the war as far as possible from the Red River delta, where the French superiority in fire power and mobility was overwhelming.

In doing this, Giap applied a cardinal principle of guerrilla warfare: The guerrilla must find the weak points in his enemy's military posture, where he is exposed and vulnerable, and seek to destroy his forces there. Another aspect of this tactic is that it gave Giap strategic mobility for his increasingly large units. Strategic mobility for a company-size unit means being able to move a few miles without interference from the enemy, but much longer distances are required for a 12,000-man division. The size of the unit that a guerrilla commander can build depends upon the size of the territory in which he can maneuver safely.

The conquest of the Thai region had given Giap shorter lines of communication with China, whence supplies were pouring in larger volume, including trucks and artillery pieces. The French tried to activate guerrillas recruited among Thai tribesmen to sever Giap's supply lines, but they never succeeded, although they constituted a serious nuisance to the Vietminh. (At one time several Chinese regiments crossed the Yünnan border to give Giap a hand against the pro-French guerrillas of Chau Quan Lo.)

By October 1952 Giap was preparing an invasion of Laos, aware that road-bound French mobile columns would not be able to pursue him there. And even if the French could drop paratroopers to stop him, aircraft would not be available to supply them indefinitely. General Salan, however, launched a powerful armored column up the Clear River valley to cut Giap's communications with his bases in the Vietbac mountains.

Initially, the French were successful; they even captured a large Vietminh weapons and ammunition depot at Phudoan. But Salan discovered what many commanders have since learned: It takes so many aircraft, helicopters and trucks to support a modern force of 30,000 men in the jungle that such offensives create an insoluble logistics problem. Perhaps one day the invention of a reliable energy cell powering tanks and heavy vehicles will relieve commanders of the drudgery of airlifting thousands of gallons of fuel.

As soon as Salan had withdrawn from the Clear River valley, Giap resumed his offensive against French enclaves in the northwest. By November's end Giap had thrown three divisions against the French "hedgehog" of Nasan, an important position on the Black River, 140 miles west of Hanoi. Garrisoned by 2,000 of the best French troops, Nasan was a tough nut to crack. The fortified hedgehog was commanded by General Jean Gilles, a paratrooper. When Vietminh troops set foot on one of the steep hills defending Nasan, Gilles launched a brutal counterattack with his paratroopers. Gilles' motto was "slash, burn, and clobber." Wherever he went he ordered his men to cut down trees to create clear fields of fire that offered the guerrillas no place to hide. His bunkers were deep and sturdy. His troops loved him. Gilles had no trouble with guerrillas at his rear. He *had* no rear. Everything was dropped to him by air, including *vinogel* (concentrated red wine). Giap failed at Nasan, leaving 5,000 of his best soldiers in the bush before the French positions, but he had learned a vital lesson of positional warfare that he was to use at Dienbienphu.

General Henri Navarre, a taciturn, publicity-shy officer who had spent most of his secretive career as an intelligence expert, was appointed commander-in-chief of French Indochina in May 1953. And once again the French worked out a plan that, it was hoped, would allow them to regain the military initiative and break up the Vietminh main force units.

As Paris sent him more reinforcements, Navarre could muster 450,000 men, of whom 120,000 were either French or Africans. The size of the Vietnamese army was brought to 290,000 men, of uneven quality. In just one year, the French trained 107 new Vietnamese Light Infantry Battalions, 95,000 men strong. Weapons and equipment were supplied by the United States. Within a few months, Navarre could field twenty-seven mobile brigades, including eighty-four battalions free from garrison duty. Within hours, any of these battalions could be airlifted anywhere in Indochina. Forty-four mobile battalions were concentrated in North Vietnam under General René Cogny, a quietly competent officer. Cogny carried out a very successful hit-and-run raid against Giap's supply depots in Langson, 80 miles northeast of Hanoi. More raids of this type would have kept Giap off balance. But Navarre, who knew little about Indochina and even less about guerrilla warfare, thought differently. Though he approved the recapture of Dienbienphu by Gilles' paratroopers, Navarre decided to open a new front in Central Vietnam to smash some of Giap's secondary guerrilla bases.

Twenty-one battalions of infantry and artillery, a total of 16,200 men, were eventually airlifted into the fortress of Dienbienphu with one general and sixteen colonels. This was only a small percentage of the 450,000 men under Navarre's command. But the Dienbienphu garrison included seven airborne battalions that Navarre should have kept in strategic reserve for quick thrusts at Giap's rear.

Here, the lesson is that a military commander should never allow his mobile reserves to become tied up in positional warfare if they cannot be removed and engaged in another tactical theater of operation within twenty-four hours. Giap's five main force divisions were entirely free to move because the task of harassing the French in the delta was entrusted to three "resident" regiments supported by some 70,000 local guerrillas. Giap regarded the activity of these guerrillas as of equal importance to the thrust of his five crack divisions. In fact, the dedicated delta guerrillas created enormous difficulties for the French along Highway 5, their main logistical line between the port of Haiphong and Hanoi. Giap later admitted that he owed his victory to the fact that two-thirds of the 450,000 French Union forces in Indochina were immobilized by the activities of his regional forces and guerrillas—a feat that the Vietcong would try to repeat later in South Vietnam.

At Dienbienphu, the French gambled on a fierce but short set-piece battle, something like a bigger Nasan. It would be tough and bloody, they thought confidently, but they could take it and inflict a beating on Giap's regulars. Instead, Giap —who had analyzed the reasons for his earlier failure at Nasan—conceived his offensive as a long, protracted campaign involving several diversionary maneuvers to confuse the French. Throughout Indochina, Giap launched five main thrusts toward Laos, Central Vietnam's highlands, and even Cambodia—forcing Navarre to scatter his mobile reserves to protect the threatened regions. Simultaneously, Vietminh commandos staged successful raids against French air bases, destroying French aircraft on the ground. Presumably at the urging of Chinese and Russian military experts who visited his headquarters at the time, Giap revived the ancient art of trench warfare; like the tentacles of an octopus, the narrow, zigzagging Vietminh trenches slowly snaked into the French strongpoints in the Dienbienphu valley, in a slow strangulation of the French positions.

To protect his ten pieces of 105-mm. artillery (in addition to about 1,000 mortars), Giap buried them deeply on the mountain slopes where neither the French air force nor counterbattery salvos were able to silence them. That artillery can be effectively protected from air strikes is one of the lessons of Dienbienphu. Another is that a large body of troops (Giap had nearly 50,000 men clustered around the valley) can be supplied by bearers and porters using every available means, from packhorses to wheelbarrows and bicycles, to haul ammunition, fuel, and food to the front. So effective was Ho Chi Minh's hold on the Vietnamese peasantry that he was able to order total mobilization of Vietnamese men and women in rural areas to supply Dienbienphu. These civilians were called *dan cong*. Perhaps Giap owes them his successes as much as he owes them to the death-volunteers who sacrificed themselves to silence French machinegun nests. Ironically, many of these *dan cong* laborers, as well as the rice they were carrying, were coming from the Red River delta, theoretically under French control.

I flew into Dienbienphu and over the forests where Giap was massing his divisions for the assault. Unbelievably, although flying low, we could not spot a single Vietminh bivouac or gun emplacement; everything was concealed under trees or underground. The dark brown jungle looked empty, and still we knew the Vietminh were there!

Giap's own command post was a 300-yard-long tunnel dug into the flank of a mountain near a cool cascade. From this comfortable hole, Giap and his youthful staff of officers planned every aspect of the battle, sometimes wondering if enough artillery and mortar shells would arrive in time for the next day's assault.

The Vietminh commander was not without problems of his own. The wear and grind on his troops was such that a few battalion commanders broke down. Even toward the end of the battle, Vietminh soldiers surrendered to the French rather than face the unbearable agony of another suicidal assault across French mine fields. With Navarre in command on the French side, Giap was blessed with an adversary who was unaware that the fate of the Indochinese war would be decided, once and forever, at Dienbienphu.

On the very day Giap made his decision to attack Dienbienphu, Navarre was launching *Opération Atlante* in the southern part of Annam, 600 miles away. The mobile reserves that Navarre committed to Atlante would have been useful to harass Giap's tenuous lines of communications. Not that it would have made much difference, as it turned out. The French did not know it then, but they had already lost Indochina in December 1950, as the first Chinese Communist soldiers reached the Vietnamese border. From that day, Vo Nguyen Giap could use China's immensity as his sanctuary, and China never would have permitted a French victory in Indochina.

Ho Chi Minh received the news of the Dienbienphu victory with a "so-what" attitude. Said Ho in a proclamation dated May 8, 1954: "This victory is big, but it is only a beginning. We must not be self-complacent, subjective nor underestimate the enemy. . . . A struggle, whether military or diplomatic, must be long and hard before complete victory can be achieved."

CHAOS IN LAOS

The kingdom of Laos—strategically located, politically complicated, and almost continuously in the international spotlight—can blame geography for many of the problems that have highlighted its short but turbulent history. If, for many countries, the end of World War II marked the beginning of an era of peace, for Laos it signaled the start of a twenty-year struggle, first for independence, then to resist foreign ideologies.

Aside from its complex governmental problems and the threats that have arisen from its proximity to China and North Vietnam, landlocked Laos has other points of vulnerability. The country is sparsely populated, with only slightly more than 3,000,000 inhabitants in an area as large as Oregon.

To use the word "undeveloped" to describe the Laotian economy is an understatement. Until recently, Laos' main export, besides $2,000,000 worth of opium to the United States, was tiger bones, traditionally used in Chinese medicine. Jungles and mountains along Laos' borders provide ideal cover for infiltrators, smugglers, and guerrillas. Because the people belong to countless ethnic groups, one of the government's most difficult tasks has been to foster a sense of nationhood among a population that has come to regard war as a natural calamity, like typhoons and plague.

Since 1945, Laos' unending guerrilla war has passed through many complicated phases. The main ones follow:

PHASE 1: Transition toward independence (1946-1949). During this period, the Lao Issara (Free Lao) was exclusively a guerrilla movement seeking to achieve independence and the end of French rule. Later, the Pathet Lao movement, led by Prince Souphanouvong and allied to the Vietminh, was unable to arouse the nationalist fervor of the Laotians by and large satisfied with the quasi-independence granted by France. In terms of fighting, nothing really significant happened in Laos until toward the end of the Indochinese war.

PHASE 2: Vietminh invasion (1953-1954). By mid-1953, the Vietminh commander-in-chief, General Vo Nguyen Giap, had decided to open a second front in Laos as part of a carefully planned diversionary maneuver before the battle of Dienbienphu, designed to mask from the French his real offensive intention. Coordinating their moves with the somewhat ineffective Pathet Lao guerrillas, elements of two elite North Vietnamese divisions attacked in the direction of Thakhet in central Laos and Attopeu in lower Laos. Taking a French regimental force by surprise along Route 12, the North Vietnamese defeated four French companies, capturing four 105-mm. howitzers. Vietminh troops invaded the fertile Bolovens Plateau and seized the isolated provincial capital of Attopeu. In northern Laos, Vietminh regiments marched toward Luang Prabang, pursuing a French column.

The lightning Vietminh offensive compelled French General Henri Navarre to divert several mobile battalions to safeguard his bases in Laos: 15 French battalions in central Laos to defend Savannakhet and the Seno airbase, and 9 battalions for Luang Prabang and the outpost of Muong Sai. The French were unable to prevent the fall of Phong Saly and of the border region with China.

But the probe against Luang Prabang was only a feint. General Giap quickly recalled his crack battalions for the assault against Dienbienphu. In Laos, the Vietminh demonstrated that a well-trained guerrilla force organized in battalions and regiments could move faster across the mountains and jungle than a relatively modern army supplied by air but encumbered by equipment and having fixed strongholds to defend. Vo Nguyen Giap called this type of operation "mobile warfare."

The French military tactic, later imitated by the Laotians, was to create fortified "hedgehogs" rapidly reinforced and supplied by air, against which the lightly armed guerrillas were expected to lose their advantage of mobility. A military hedgehog is a defensive stronghold shaped like a porcupine and fortified with barbed wire, minefields, pillboxes, and concentration of artillery for sustained resistance to frontal attacks. Years later, U.S. Marines temporarily created a typical hedgehog at Khesanh, a small valley commanding a major invasion route from Laos.

In practice, the French were able to hold a hedgehog located in a good defensive position as long as they could land C-47 aircraft to bring in supplies and fresh troops and to evacuate the wounded. At Sam Neua, Nam Bac, Phong Saly, and other places in Laos, Vietminh troops making a judicious use of mortar fire were able to interdict the airstrips to French aircraft. The isolated French and Laotian garrisons (one or two battalions) had either to flee or to surrender. Unlike the Vietminh regulars, French army units were not trained to fight mobile battles in the jungle.

The guerrilla war in roadless Laos followed the valleys, which are the natural lines of communications and the only populated regions of the country. In the valleys, the Vietminh soldiers could obtain rice to feed themselves and porters to carry their ammunition. They could use canoes and bamboo rafts to transport heavier loads. They had positioned ammunition dumps in advance of their troops. Whoever controls the valleys in Laos controls most of the population of the country.

PHASE 3: Regroupment and politics (1954-1959). Following the Geneva Conference came the phase of regroupment for the guerrillas and the transformation of the Pathet Lao into a political organization known as the Neo Lao Hak Xat. Fighting was limited to harassment of outposts in the two northern provinces of Phong Saly and Sam Neua until the integration of Pathet Lao units into the Royal Laotian Army.

PHASE 4: Three-way war (1960-1962). Using their alliance with the neutralist forces of Captain Kong Le, Pathet Lao guerrillas resumed offensive operations throughout Laos, enlisting the support of local tribes. From that period, the Pathet Lao units were openly supported by Hanoi and organized on the model of the North Vietnamese army. The fighting stopped in 1962 after the Geneva Conference divided Laos into two spheres of influence: a United States-influenced area in the Mekong Valley and a Communist area along the border with Vietnam and China.

PHASE 5: Royalist gains (1965-1967). Increased to 60,000 men, strengthened by American equipment, and backed by the U.S. Air Force flying from Udon in Thailand, the Royalist army gained superiority both in firepower and mobility over the Pathet Lao guerrillas. The clearing operations conducted by the Royalists dislodged the guerrillas from Champassak and Sayabouri provinces, the only two Laotian provinces on the west side of the Mekong River. Pathet Lao positions were weakened in the vicinity of the Plain of Jars, and although they still controlled the plain itself, Route 7, the only supply line with North Vietnam, became vulnerable to continual harassment by Meo guerrillas operating from the hills and supplied by Air America, financed by the Central Intelligence Agency.

In the south, the Pathet Lao were pushed back from the Mekong valley along the entire panhandle of Laos, all the way from Thakhet to Pakse. The Royal Laotian government control extended as far as the inland towns of Saravane and Attopeu, beyond the Bolovens Plateau. The success of these mopping-up operations was attributed to the constant United States air support and to the Pathet Lao's own inability to recruit more guerrillas outside of the tribal groups.

In December 1965, a North Vietnamese force estimated at regiment size participated in an attack on the Laotian Army Officers School at Dong Hene, near Savannakhet, in central Laos. According to Laotian sources, the attack was in connection with the infiltration of a group of guerrillas into northeast Thailand, across the Mekong River. Several North Vietnamese regulars were captured.

By mid-1967, Hanoi had escalated the little war in Laos (which became a sideshow to the more serious fighting in Vietnam) by increasing its own commitment to some 40,000 men. Perhaps 25,000 of these were strung in defensive positions along the Ho Chi Minh Trail to South Vietnam. In January 1968 other North Vietnamese forces coming from the direction of the Dienbienphu valley overran the Laotian resistance position held by four *groupes mobiles* at Nam Bac, 60 miles north of Luang Prabang. (A Laotian *groupe mobile* (GM) is roughly the equivalent of a U.S. regimental combat team composed of two or three infantry battalions supported by an artillery battery and some service units.) Presumably, North Vietnamese forces opened this "second front" in northern Laos to aid their hard-pressed

Pathet Lao ally in other areas. Eventually, Nam Bac was captured by the Communists. Everywhere, the guerrillas were on the offensive in Laos while Giap mounted his daring Tet offensive in South Vietnam.

The government in Vientiane produced 11 North Vietnamese military defectors. Forty other North Vietnamese, claimed the government, had been captured in Laos since September 1956. Each month, the shadowy war in Laos claims about 100 victims among government forces and perhaps 300 among Pathet Lao and North Vietnamese troops. Half of the country, containing perhaps 1,000,000 inhabitants under Pathet Lao political control, has become a "free strike" zone for U.S. jets and Royalist T-28 fighter bombers. The overwhelming majority of "combat" casualties are inflicted by artillery, mortars, and air strikes, as foot soldiers rarely come face to face in the immensity of the Laotian jungle. One observer in Vientiane described the North Vietnamese battalions infiltrated into Laos as "big submarines, hiding and moving under the canopy of the jungle, then surfacing unexpectedly 100 miles away to strike at their objective." "We have not yet learned how to detect them when they are immersed," he added.

Perhaps the most successful counterguerrilla operation mounted by the United States in Asia since the end of World War II is that of the Meo *maquis* afield in the remote mountains of northern Laos. Led by a popular Meo chieftain known as General Vang Pao, the Meo bands consist mainly of American-equipped tribesmen stiffened with a sprinkling of U.S. "advisers."

The Meo, who are of Sino-Tibetan origin, are tough hardy warriors who wear massive silver necklaces both as badge of honor and amulet. In their hilltop villages the Meo men—

when not at war—wear a sort of blue uniform and a black beret. They are so fiercely independent that no administration—French, Laotian, or Communist—has ever managed to control them effectively. On the cool mountain slopes, Meo women cultivate the white poppy from which opium is extracted. By mysterious channels, the raw opium is smuggled to the rest of Southeast Asia, and to the United States after transformation into heroin.

Meo loyalty to the Vientiane government has been sealed since 1962 by an airlift of rice, rifles, and grenades delivered by a fleet of small, unmarked aircraft. During the dry winter season, the courier planes land on narrow airstrips carved out of forests near Meo villages. When the slopes are too steep to permit safe landing, supplies are dropped by parachute.

In the provinces of Xieng Khouang and Sam Neua, General Vang Pao has created a strong political and military organization that seriously hampers the Pathet Lao units engaged in guerrilla war against the Vientiane government. Frequently, Meo tribesmen carry out hit-and-run attacks against isolated North Vietnamese vehicles hauling supplies for Prince Souphanouvong's Pathet Lao army. The Meo are at their best fighting within their own territory on the mountain ridges.

For two years the U.S. airlift has helped to support and feed some 160,000 Meo tribesmen, in payment for their guerrilla activities that have pinned down several Pathet Lao and North Vietnamese battalions in defense of their lines of communications around Sam Neua. In the foothills bordering the Plain of Jars, well-armed Meo fighters pose a serious threat to Pathet Lao supply routes and outposts. Bridges are blown up, sentries captured or slain. Because of Meo support, U.S. aircraft and helicopters are able to land on at least a dozen airstrips deep behind Pathet Lao lines, sometimes only a stone's throw from the North Vietnamese border.

To fight the Meo threat, the Pathet Lao have planted thousands of mines on the spider web of dirt trails converging toward the streams where the Meo obtain water. Victims have been many. Young amputees are a frequent sight in Meo villages. The Pathet Lao claims to have "liquidated" 1,300 Meo "bandits" in the province of Sam Neua during the first three months of 1967, a claim impossible to verify. Smaller pockets of Meo resistance fighters are also active in the mountains north of Luang Prabang.

A dissident Meo group, including perhaps 40,000 tribesmen and led by a rival chieftain called Phay Dang, fights— with much less success—on the Pathet Lao side around the plateau of Xieng Khouang.

In February 1968, the reorganized Laotian People's Liberation Army and its North Vietnamese allies decided to strike a lethal blow at General Vang Pao's guerrillas. March 11: the last Special Forces camp at Pa Thi was overrun: It was a vital position from which pro-U.S. guerrillas had conducted harassment raids against Pathet Lao garrisons and communications in the three northern provinces contiguous to China and to North Vietnam. Then a large number of Communist troops moved against the positions held by the rightists on the southern fringe of the Plain of Jars. Three Royal Laotian battalions were flushed out of their hill-top positions in the Munong Ngan area.

Pushing south, the Pathet Lao army occupied the strategically important areas of Tha Thom and Tha Vieng, on the road to Paksane on the Mekong River. This left Luang Prabang completely isolated and at the mercy of Pathet Lao raids against its airfield, where Royalist planes were periodically put out of action by saboteurs. Bitter at the lack of U.S.

support, General Vang Pao pulled back the remnants of his Meo guerrillas to the fortress of Sam Thong, the last military garrison standing between the Pathet Lao and Prince Souvanna Phouma's administrative capital in Vientiane.

At the time, U.S. intelligence estimated that there were 70,000 North Vietnamese regulars in Laos, an all-time record number. Several thousands of them were on their way to South Vietnam, but Hanoi intelligently made use of their passage through Laos to lend a charitable hand to its Pathet Lao allies. As an added benefit, the Laos operation offered the Hanoi generals a chance to train and test unseasoned troops against a relatively weak adversary before the much harder encounters awaiting them in Vietnam.

In lower Laos, the NVA-Pathet Lao forces smashed into the Royalist stronghold of Lao Ngam, defended by the 802nd Royal Lao Regiment, on the Bolovens Plateau, 20 miles southwest of Attopeu. By this time, all the Royalist positions remaining in southern Laos—Tha Teng, Attopeu, and Saravane—were practically under siege by the Laotian People's Liberation Army. Officially, there was no war in Laos. But, using patient guerrilla tactics, the Pathet Lao had gradually extended its control over two-thirds of the country, opening a strategic corridor of infiltration stretching 600 miles from China's Yünnan to Cambodia and to South Vietnam.

CAMBODIA'S DIFFICULT NEUTRALITY

Norodom Sihanouk became king of Cambodia on April 25, 1941, at the age of 18. His country was then under French protectorate which it had been since 1863. Sihanouk's reign as king lasted fourteen eventful years. He resigned in 1955 to become Prince Sihanouk, Chief of State.

It is April, the hottest month in Cambodia. The young

prince in his palace receives confusing reports of peasants' unrest—reports that come from a remote region named Samlaut, not too far from the sapphire mines of Pailin. There is no telephone communication with the impoverished district of Samlaut. The distance from the capital of Phnom Penh is only 180 miles, yet it would take at least ten hours to drive there. The entire kingdom has but five helicopters; at the moment none is available. Maps are consulted. On most of them the name of Samlaut is absent. Apparently, the only way to get there is by jeep or oxcart, on a dirt trail.

Finally, the worried prince obtains a telegram from his military commander in Samlaut detailing the situation. For no apparent reason, several thousand local peasants—coarse, barefooted men and women in sarongs—attacked an outpost of the provincial guard, stealing weapons from the twenty-five frightened militiamen. The village chief named Pen Ly, and some other minor officials, were massacred by the insurgents armed with shotguns, spears and hunting knives. Then the angered peasants, among whom several saffron-robed monks were seen, marched to a small rice farm recently opened by the government. They burned down its modest buildings. The fields around were worked by a group of "Yuvans," a pro-government youth organization, who had cleared the surrounding forest to grow food.

The prince flashes an alarm signal to his army; two elite battalions of paratroopers are rushed to the troubled spot. But the prince is confused. He vaguely recalls that fifteen years before, during the Indochina war—he was then a very young king—the forests around Pailin were the refuge of Khmer Vietminh—small insurgent bands who said they were fighting the French army. The Khmer Vietminh were the allies of Ho Chi Minh, the chief of all revolution-

AGE OF THE GUERRILLA

aries in Indochina. The prince asks himself, "Why would my peasants revolt against me today? Aren't we independent? There are no more colonial troops to fight. Don't they know my name? I am Norodom Sihanouk, the former king and today the Chief of State, the one that 6,000,000 Cambodians call the Father of the Independence!" Silent remain the forests, save for the scattered explosions of gunshots.

The prince receives a report from his battalions sent against the rebels. The report explains that as the paratroopers arrived in Samlaut, local peasants fled into the forest after burning down a bridge and their own thatched houses. The soldiers arrested forty-eight rebels, who confessed that they had attacked the provincial guards to steal their weapons. They also confessed that they had acted on the orders of "their big leaders" in the capital.

The peasants of Samlaut accuse the prince of having betrayed the nation and of accepting the return of thousands of Frenchmen in Phnom Penh. During the Indochina war five battalions of French forces were stationed in Cambodia. The prince declares that he has only 300 Frenchmen to train his small army of 47,000 men equipped with weapons offered by several socialist countries, including Russia and China.

The peasants also accused the prince's government of using the pretext of building a new farm to clear the forests to prepare landing strips for U.S. helicopters to land troops. "Absurd," says the prince. "We clear the forests only to make more cultivable land and certainly not to serve the Americans. We don't even have diplomatic relations with the Americans, who help the Thais and the Vietnamese, the traditional enemies of our peaceful Buddhist country."

The prince sends five of his infantry battalions to reinforce the paratroopers sweeping the forests in vain pursuit

of the elusive rebels. The capital is abuzz with rumors that
250 rebels have already been killed. Students demonstrate in
the streets, demanding that Lon Nol, the prime minister, be
fired. Lon Nol—the former chief of the prince's army—is
accused of being secretly pro-American. Leftist deputies in
the parliament regard Lon Nol—a professional soldier—as
their sworn enemy.

Leftist newspapers—subsidized by foreign embassies—
clamor for closer ties between Cambodia and the Communist governments in Hanoi and Peking. They would like the
prince to openly support the Vietcong guerrillas, who are
fighting the Americans in South Vietnam, a country with
whom Cambodia shares an uneasy border.

The prince goes on the radio and states: "The nation must
conduct military operations to repress the revolt of the
Khmer Reds who have caused bloodshed in the country.
These operations must be carried out because I received reports that the Khmer Reds have burned a bridge built by
our government. These bridges belong to the people and to
the state. I want to inform my compatriots that of the forty-
eight rebels who have been captured, we will release those
who have been misled. Those who attacked the provincial
guards will be sent before the military tribunal for trial."
A few days later, the prince learns that the insurgents number about 300 armed men and receive assistance from 2,000
local supporters.

One month goes by. In Phnom Penh, two leftwing deputies named Hou Yuon and Khieu Samphan mysteriously
disappear from their homes. Hu Nimh, a young, bright pro-
Communist deputy, accuses the Lon Nol government of
having kidnapped, and perhaps killed, his two friends; but
the police suspect that the pair went underground, perhaps
to lead the rebellion with some forty male and female school

teachers who have abandoned their class rooms for the Communist underground. Hu Nimh, a gentle-looking intellectual, is popular among the leftist students in Phnom Penh, but the prince considers him a dangerous man, a man to watch.

In May, the prince visits his astrologers before making new decisions. Every year, before the coming of the planting season, sacred bulls are consulted. In Angkor (a thousand years ago Angkor was the center of the magnificent Khmer Empire), the prince leads two bulls covered with gold and silver into a field where plates containing the country's most important resources are lined up on the ground. One plate contains rice; a second, water; a third, grass; a fourth, wheat; a fifth, corn; and a sixth, alcohol. The prince leads the bulls to the plates, then releases them. That crop will fail which is most eaten by the bulls. One year the bulls ate most from the plate containing rice, whereupon the prince's government—anticipating a bad crop—banned all rice exports. This anecdote illustrates how vastly the Cambodian response to life and its problems differs from a Western response. And it is in view of a non-Western response to life that one must view the steps taken by Prince Sihanouk to quell the Samlaut rebellion.

When, after the coming of the first rains, the army seems unable to restore order in Samlaut, and the unrest—though still limited—threatens to spread elsewhere in the kingdom, the prince recalls the troops to their barracks. Rebels who were captured are freed. The provincial officials, whom the peasants accused of doing nothing for the people, are replaced.

The prince takes his helicopter and flies to Samlaut, tells the peasants that his government will create schools and infirmaries. He will give money to restore their pagodas.

The prince kneels on the ground in front of elderly Buddhist monks and begs them to ask the peasants to leave the forests and return to their village; that everything is forgotten. Then, the prince dismisses the controversial Lon Nol and forms a new government, in which two pro-Peking leftists are included. By the end of the month of June, the prince tells his people that "peace and harmony" have returned to Cambodia.

This is not a fiction story from Shangri-La. It is the account with precise details of a recent guerrilla outbreak in the kingdom of Cambodia, a relaxed and cheerful country best remembered as the locale of the magnificent temples of Angkor Wat. Almost completely surrounded by Thailand, Laos, and South Vietnam, Cambodia would prefer to be left alone by its turbulent neighbors. But with the ideological conflict raging in Southeast Asia and the war in South Vietnam, this dream seems hardly possible.

Although Cambodia's perennial ruler, Prince Norodom Sihanouk, tries to observe a difficult neutrality, his country is increasingly affected by the Vietnamese war. The United States, South Vietnam, and the Vietcong are all exerting pressures to shake Cambodia out of its fragile neutrality and move it into their own camps.

Some U.S. officials have charged that Cambodian territory already serves as staging area and supply center for at least 15,000 Vietcong guerrillas operating in the Vietnamese highlands. With a small land army of 29,000 men, Cambodia can do little to prevent the better-armed Vietcong regiments from hiding in its jungle.

In Vietnam, U.S. officials have repeatedly denounced the presence of an important Vietcong command in Cambodia's roadless Ratanakiri Province. It is believed that either

by smuggling or other means, Vietcong purchasing agents
obtain each year 40,000 tons of rice, medicines and some
other products in Cambodia. Traditionally, contraband has
always gone on in the border region.

The prince interpreted the Samlaut affair as a signal from
his leftwing opposition that he should replace Prime Minister Lon Nol with another man, more "acceptable" to Hanoi
and Peking. The shrewd prince accepted this "political solution" to the crisis, but four months later he dumped the leftist ministers from the cabinet and cracked down on Maoist
political activists suspected of trying to introduce the "Cultural Revolution" among Cambodia's Chinese—who number approximately half a million.

In addition to denouncing the leftwing intellectuals in
Phnom Penh, the prince has often attacked, as a source of
subversion, Cambodia's small Pracheachon (Communist)
Party, whose present leader is Non Suon. Non Suon's followers—estimated at about 1,000—undoubtedly are in close
contact with Vietcong agents operating in Cambodia. Several hundred Khmer guerrilla leaders have received training
in North Vietnam since the end of the Indochina war in
1954.

From the right, Prince Sihanouk is facing yet another
guerrilla threat in the form of the *Khmer Serei* (the Free
Khmer). Their leader, Son Ngoc Thanh, was Cambodian
prime minister during the Japanese occupation and shortly
afterwards. Thanh, who is traveling between Saigon and
Bangkok, is a long-time rival of Prince Sihanouk and supports the abolition of Cambodia's constitutional monarchy.
Cambodian army intelligence estimates Khmer Serei guerrillas operating from Thailand at 600 men. In South Vietnam, the Khmer Serei number between 2,000 and 3,000
men, many of whom have volunteered for the U.S.-trained
C.I.D.G. (Civilian Irregulars Defense Groups).

Prince Sihanouk has accused Thailand, with whom he broke diplomatic relations several years ago, and the U.S., of supporting and arming the Khmer Serei, who are particularly active in six western provinces along the Thai Cambodia border. Khmer Serei guerrillas have attacked small Cambodian outposts and laid mines on roads and trails to protect their bases. Apparently, however, they do not enjoy much active popular support inside Cambodia.

THAILAND, THE NEXT TARGET

"Thailand is the next target for Liberation. . . ."

Marshal Chen Yi
January 1, 1965

Thailand is a Buddhist kingdom with a population of approximately 32,000,000 and an area slightly larger than that of Spain. The Bangkok metropolitan area has a population of over 2,000,000. The overwhelming majority of the Thai people are farmers who own their land. Although per capita income is low, there is no serious deprivation of the necessities of life that would threaten the country's social stability.

Other factors working for stability are the unusually high degree of linguistic and religious unity among the population, the universal respect for the monarchy, and a well-established civil service. The relative strength of Thailand's institutions is no doubt a reflection of the country's cohesion over six centuries of independence, and the continuity in the monarchy, the present king, Bhumibol, having descended in unbroken line from the first Chakri ruler, who assumed the throne in 1782. Although since 1932 the king has not wielded real political power, he remains an important symbol of unity and central authority.

Some 3,000,000 Chinese in Thailand constitute the largest

alien minority. Prominent in the country's economic life, they have profited from the absence of serious religious, cultural, or racial discrimination and enjoy good relations with the Thais. Quite a few Thai leaders are known to have Chinese blood. There is no evidence that Thailand's Chinese, who often use Thai names and have taken Thai citizenship, are supporting the guerrillas in any way.

Since 1964 there has been a marked step-up in subversive activity directed against Thailand as Thailand more and more is used by the United States to further the war effort in Vietnam. The government has reacted to this challenge with vigor and has directed a major portion of its resources and energy to containing and stifling the insurgency in parts of the northeast and in the south.

Attempts to subvert Thailand are by no means new. A Chinese-sponsored "Free Thai Movement" with the announced purpose of overthrowing the Thai government was formed in the early 1950's and was associated with a "Thai Autonomous Area" maintained by the Chinese regime in Yünnan Province. When this proved ineffective, Chinese efforts were directed toward developing a separatist movement in northeast Thailand. This effort failed as well, and Communist activity slowed in 1963, although Peking continued a virulent propaganda campaign against the pro-American Thai leaders.

In November 1964, Peking and Hanoi announced the formation of the Thailand Independence Movement (TIM), and a clandestine radio outside Thailand called the "Voice of the Thai People" intensified its propaganda aimed at the subversion of Thailand. In January 1965, Peking announced the formation of the Thai Patriotic Front and the subsequent merger of the TIM with the TPF, which plays a role analogous to that of the National Liberation Front in Vietnam. In early 1966, the TPF announced that its goal was the destruction of "U.S. imperialists and their lackeys," and that this required enlarging the "armed struggle" in Thailand into "a people's war."

There appears to be only moderate popular support for these front groups in Thailand. But the familiar combination of terror and assassination combined with promises and propaganda has been growing, particularly in the northeast. In 1965 occurred the first clash between Thai security patrols and an armed band. There have since been more than 800 such clashes, usually precipitated by increasingly aggressive patrolling by Thai government forces. Other clashes have been an outgrowth of Communist efforts to embarrass or impede government psychological and developmental programs. Government officials have been ambushed.

The number of active insurgents is small. They operate in hilly and thinly populated territory in the most remote parts of the country. The Thai government recognizes that the absence of close links with the remote areas is a principal weakness, and a major effort is being made to establish an effective and strong government presence. The plan involves a combination of quick-impact service operations in the area most affected by the insurgency and longer-range programs for the betterment of living conditions throughout the less developed areas. At the same time the government is making a major effort to improve security, communications, and intelligence in the insurgency-affected area.

In 1967, some 36,000 U.S. military personnel were deployed in Thailand to back up the U.S. military effort in South Vietnam as well as to advise the Thais in their own counterguerrilla drive. Of these, 8,000 Army engineers were engaged in the construction of 500 miles of strategic roads, communications networks, port facilities, military supply depots, and other installations. Two-thirds of the Americans in Thailand are Air Force men flying or servicing 300 to 400 planes that take off from eight major Thai bases such as Khorat, Ubon, and Takli to bomb North Vietnam and the Ho Chi Minh Trail in Laos. At Nakhon Phanon, a maximum-security base in the Mekong Valley, the 606th Air Commando Squadron flies secret counterinsurgency missions over Laos.

Since May 1967, giant B-52 bombers have begun operating from the U Tapao airbase's new 11,500-feet runway, the longest in Southeast Asia. This means that the big planes no longer need make a 4,500-mile round trip from Guam to hit their targets in Vietnam. At a cost of $90,000,000, the United States has built a new port complex at Sattahip, a short distance from U Tapao.

Clearly intending to help the Thais nip their guerrilla problem in the bud, the United States has provided Thailand's 80,000-man armed forces with $672,000,000 in military aid since 1950 and is stepping up 1968 spending to $60,000,000. In addition, it has poured in $450,000,000 in economic aid in the past seventeen years. Overall, the United States is now spending more than $100,000,000 a year in Thailand to prevent another Vietnam. But will it work?

Facts about the insurgency in northeast Thailand are as hard to track down as its elusive guerrillas. One can drive 500 miles on country roads without seeing any evidence of the fighting. Yet more than a hundred village officials and government informers have been assassinated in this placid landscape. Physically, the countryside looks like the driest part of Oklahoma. Smallish dipterocarp trees dot the infertile soil of sandy loam. The checkerboard of diked paddies appears empty under the broiling sun. The rare vehicles on the roads raise curtains of red dust.

Though it produces 35 percent of the rice exported by Thailand, the northeast badly lacks water during the dry months. The summer monsoon brings flash floods that erode the soil. One-third of Thailand's inhabitants live there in six provinces bulging toward Laos and Cambodia. Their annual per capita income of $60 is about half the national average. The fact that American money "buys" politicians and bureaucrats in the cities and ignores the poor is one factor that suggests the United States may be wasting over $100,000,000 a year in Thailand.

Until recently, the government in Bangkok had demonstrated little interest in this tropical Siberia, totally lacking in industries. The northeast was originally peopled by Lao prisoners of war brought in during the 18th century, when Thailand nearly absorbed its smaller neighbor. The peasant there is regarded somewhat as a spoiler by the more prosperous farmer of the lush Central Plain, who pays more attention to irrigation and other modern agricultural practices.

In a series of verdant villages along the wide Mekong River live 40,000 North Vietnamese, vegetable farmers and craftsmen who fled Laos in 1946 as French troops reoccupied Indochina. Their loyalty is to Hanoi. Even in the absence of direct participation in the insurgency, there is little doubt that the industrious Vietnamese provide some assistance to the guerrillas operating in the close-by Pu Pan hills. The district of Nagae, not far from the U.S. airbase of Nakhon Phanon, is highly susceptible to infiltration from North Vietnam across the narrow waist of guerrilla-infested Laos. Reportedly, the staging area for the infiltrators is in the village of Mahaxai, in central Laos. For the moment, the guerrillas are more interested in establishing their political con-

trol over isolated *mubans* (villages) than in challenging the
Thai army in set-piece battles. There are 41,630 *mubans* in
Thailand.

The ultimate solution to the unrest in the northeast is a
better way of life for the peasants, who live without electric-
ity or even water for irrigation of a worn-out soil. An ambitious project, supported by the United Nations, is under way
to dam the Mekong at Pamong. The giant multipurpose
dam is designed to provide enough irrigation water and
power for most of the northeast. It will take twenty years
and perhaps a billion dollars to achieve the project, if the
Thais have the patience, and if the American presence has
not proved more costly than the Thai politicians expect,
with the result that in less than twenty years Thailand
may find herself involved in a massive guerrilla war on her
own soil.

Though the dusty northeast receives most of the attention, it is not the only troubled spot in Thailand. The others:

In northern Thailand, guerrillas have recently spread their
activities to the mountainous province of Nam, contiguous
to Laos' Sayabouri Province. North Vietnamese and Pathet
Lao agents coming from across the Mekong River have distributed transistor radios to local Meo tribesmen so that they
can listen to propaganda broadcasts from Hanoi and Peking.
There are 80,000 Meos living in northern Thailand, 700 of
whom have joined the rebellion.

In southern Thailand, 1,000,000 Muslims of Malay origin
resent the presence of Thai functionaries from the Central
Plain. Some of the dark-skinned Muslims, who object to being treated as second-class citizens by Thai officials, support
a Malayan National Liberation League. Reportedly, the
league has joined the insurgent Thai Independence Movement, itself part of the Peking-backed Patriotic Front of

Thailand. The Malay autonomist movement in Thailand, of course, receives no support from the Malaysian government, which cooperates with the Thais in patrolling the common border.

Near the border with Malaysia, in Yala Province, some 500 hard-core Chinese terrorists—who fled Malaya in 1960, after the failure of their 12-year insurrection—are surviving in small groups scattered in the dense jungle. The Chinese, still led by Chin Peng, have been attacking Thai police outposts. They live from taxes levied on small rubber plantations operated by Chinese farmers. The Thai police are inactive in the region, where bandits make the countryside insecure.

In the narrow Kra Isthmus, a new front has been recently activated by leftist revolutionaries in the heavily forested Kui Buri District, 125 miles south of Bangkok. In September 1967, guerrillas using land mines and sub-machine guns ambushed and wiped out a 10-man Thai patrol watching the long border with Burma. Among the victims was Lieutenant Colonel Chalermwatan, the highest-ranking Thai official to have been killed, so far, by the terrorists. It was the fourth significant attack within two months in this region. Earlier, in January 1967, Thai paratroopers searching the Thai-Burma border uncovered a training camp in the mountains, and 122 insurgents were later arrested.

To counter the guerrilla threat, the Thai government of Prime Minister Thanom Kittikachorn can field no more than 130,000 men—one-fifth the size of the South Vietnamese army for a country three times larger. Of these, 80,000 are regular infantrymen, 32,000 are field policemen scattered in 72 provinces and 4,926 *tambols* (counties); 6,500 border policemen are deployed along 2,000 miles of frontier with four countries: Malaya, Burma, Laos, and

Cambodia, every one of them with its own guerrilla problem. In September 1967, the Thai government sent the "Queen Cobras," a 2,200-man expeditionary regiment, and small contingents of the navy and air force to South Vietnam, mainly for combat experience. Some 365 U.S. Special Forces men, operating from jungle camps, are teaching Thai soldiers basic counterguerrilla skills.

So far, however, most of the counterinsurgency effort has been carried on by police units. General Praphas Charusathira, commander-in-chief of the army and Interior Minister—a tough, flamboyant professional soldier—has the power to take all measures necessary to combat the guerrillas who are active in 29 provinces.

With massive United States financial assistance, the Thais are setting up Mobile Reserve Platoons and Special Action Forces in rural areas to reinforce villages that need help. Villages in the northeast have been saturated with 1,700 two-way radios that local officials can use to call for help when attacked. The system, which looks good on paper, has not in practice given the expected results; either the reinforcements arrive too late or the village chief does not dare to radio, either for fear of reprisals or because he sympathizes with the guerrillas.

Admittedly, despite massive United States support, the Thais have not been able to prevent the insurgency from growing at a disquieting pace. The fighting has now reached the level of violence that existed in South Vietnam in 1959, when the Vietcong were dismissed as a mere nuisance by senior U.S. military advisers.

Best intelligence sources estimate the guerrilla force at around 2,000 armed men—guerrillas who can count on the support of some 30,000 sympathizers, including village chiefs and local police.

The guerrillas operate in cadres of 25 to 100 men, lightly armed with rifles, automatic weapons, and some mortars. Neighboring Laos constitutes an inexhaustible source of armament for the guerrillas, who fade away into the forests when pressed too closely by the Thai army. Bangkok officials claim that each year an average of 600 Thai insurgent cadres are trained in camps located in North Vietnam, Laos, and China's Yünnan Province. And the training operation has been going on for the past seven years. The Bangkok government has repeatedly charged that Communist helicopters, presumably flying from bases in Laos or North Vietnam, are ferrying supplies to guerrillas operating in the northeast. In October 1967, the Thai government offered a reward of $10,000 (U.S.) to anyone who could down or capture on the ground one of the mysterious helicopters.

One characteristic of the Thai situation is that the three or four spots known to serve as bases for guerrilla bands are widely scattered. Without permanent liaison between them, they operate quite independently. The Nagae District, for example, lies more than 1,000 miles from the pro-Chinese Yala Province in the south. Local leaders of the rebellion in the field are mostly unknown.

As late as 1966, most observers in booming Bangkok thought that the presence of a respected king and strong Buddhist traditions among the Thais would "immunize" the country against revolutionary violence. However, the massive American presence in Thailand and the great gulf between the rich and the poor have forced the Thais to realize that they are no longer "safe" from revolution.

CHAPTER 7

VIETNAM: THE ENEMY IS EVERYWHERE AND NOWHERE

The war in Vietnam has no front lines; strategists cannot measure gains or losses by shifting colored pins around a map. In this half-guerrilla, half-conventional war, the enemy is both everywhere and nowhere.

For an idea of this hard-to-define, nearly frontless situation, one might toss a handful of red beads on a crescent-shaped map of the war-torn country. Where the beads fall would mark the location of forty or so Vietcong guerrilla bases. Then, between the beads, draw the delicate outline of a spider web—the vulnerable roads connecting cities and towns held by the South Vietnamese government—some 200 of them.

All the rest is contested area, sometimes visited by government troops, more frequently by the guerrillas. As a last touch to this surrealist war map, approximately thirty yellow beads placed along the coast and between the red beads would indicate the sea-girded enclaves and the inland bases garrisoned by U.S. forces. No wonder, then, that real situation maps of the Vietnamese war look like psychedelic posters.

It is not only from the standpoint of territory that this war is hard to measure. Other traditional war indicators are either irrelevant or suspect. A basic question, such as "How many guerrillas are we fighting?" is well-nigh impossible to answer. According to General William C. Westmoreland, just prior to his replacement by General Creighton Abrams, there were some 242,000 active Vietcong, including 115,000 regulars and part-time irregulars, plus 55,000 infiltrators from North Vietnam. Captured Vietcong documents list 100,000 regulars, 180,000 provincial troops, and 160,000 village guerrillas and militia, making a total of 440,000 men.

The best estimate of the Vietcong's fighting strength is 163 battalions of 600 men each; this is its combat power for attacks and does not include its vast political resources. In addition, the Vietcong lists 100,000 party members and another 100,000 members of "front" organizations such as Liberation Youth, Women's, and Farmers' associations. Perhaps as many as 5,000,000 Vietnamese farmers, living in 1,250 villages and 8,000 smaller hamlets over which the Saigon administration has no permanent control, are associated in one way or another with the guerrillas. The Vietcong has trusted agents in these silent villages where the 100,000 party activists constitute the guerrillas' shadow government and their political infrastructure.

Let us take Badua, a typical, palm-shaded, rice-growing village in the Mekong delta, which has been under Vietcong influence for the past five years. Everyone in Badua, willy-nilly, is contributing to the Vietcong war effort; if not as a fighter, then as a carrier of supplies, as a food producer, or as a taxpayer if he owns land. Periodically, able-bodied men leave the village for a month or two and walk as far as the Cambodian border with Vietcong guides. There they receive heavy crates of weapons, which they carry by night to a guerrilla base somewhere in the jungle.

The guerrilla fighter—as a rule—carries only his weapon and his food. The hauling and lugging is done by the *dan cong,* the hungry army of anonymous peasants drafted from their villages to handle the crude logistics of the guerrilla movement. If captured by government or American soldiers, they are thrown in jail, or even tortured. Still, a defenseless farmer could hardly refuse an order from the guerrillas—or for that matter, one from his American or Vietnamese torturers.

In Badua, there is no such thing as a neutral man, woman, or child; everyone plays a role in the guerrilla activities. Those too young, too old, or too weak to fight, fashion vicious bamboo spikes contaminated with excrement, or they spy on the government forces and warn the Vietcong when soldiers approach the village.

In other areas, as in the humid Camau Peninsula where the guerrillas have controlled the countryside for a decade, the Vietcong has established a viable society with its own primary schools, infirmaries, and even courts to settle disputes among peasants. Rice fields have been confiscated from absentee landlords and distributed to the poorest peasants whose sons have joined the guerrillas. When government troops move in, they are greeted by the hostile stares and sullen faces of villagers who regard them as intruders, if not enemies.

Unquestionalby, it is at the grass-roots level, in villages and hamlets, that the Vietcong organization is strongest. In villages under its control the Vietcong has organized "elections" for administrative committees in which only Vietcong supporters were asked to participate. Usually, these

Vietcong-elected officials are natural leaders of their community, with a better education than the average peasant. Their authority is quite similar to that of village chiefs in other parts of the country: to arbitrate quarrels among farmers and collect taxes for the Vietcong war effort. If weapons are available, a squad or a platoon of militiamen is recruited among the village's youth. Even the bashful unmarried girls are invited to join. A captured United States carbine becomes the symbol of their emancipation. Women, either as fighters or supporters, have an important place in the guerrilla organization.

At the beginning of the insurrection, between 1958 and 1960, the guerrillas manufactured their own crude weapons: single-shot pistols, bolt-action rifles, and even a small mortar fashioned from a steel pipe, which—because of its odd shape —was called the "praying mantis." Now that weapons, either captured from the Americans or smuggled from North Vietnam, are plentiful, Vietcong armories still continue to turn out grenades, mines, and a bewildering variety of booby traps—the essential weapons of guerrilla warfare. In some cases, low-flying American helicopters have even been hit by arrows shot by mountain tribesmen won over to the Vietcong cause. Bear traps are used by the guerrillas of Central Vietnam. Anything can make a weapon.

The Vietcong policy in regions under its rule, once the government agents have been eliminated, is to "arm all the people." Small militia and guerrilla groups are trained to operate within their community, provide armed support to Vietcong officials, and eventually discourage the landlords' return. Roads and trails connecting the village with the nearest government-held district capital are destroyed. The village, isolated from the rest of the country, becomes another small base for the guerrillas.

In 1962 the South Vietnamese government decided on the

construction of 17,000 "strategic hamlets" throughout the country. Each hamlet was to build fences to prevent the nightly infiltration of guerrillas seeking food or recruits, or simply to propagandize the peasants. The Saigon government provided the villagers with millions of miles of barbed wire and thousands of steel poles, as well as cement, to build their defenses. The United States contributed $10,000,000 to the program. It was a fiasco.

The plan failed for the main reason that once the fortifications were built, villagers either did not have the motivation to resist Vietcong infiltration or they were Vietcong sympathizers. In some areas, the local Vietcong cells became "fenced in" with the villagers. As soon as the government force turned its back, these Vietcong cells mobilized the farmers to destroy the fences. As the Saigon government learned later, it is useless to fence in a village unless military forces are present to guard the fences.

In answer to the government's strategic hamlets, the Vietcong countered with its own scheme of "combat hamlets." Here, there was no need for barbed wire or other costly devices: the Vietcong used only locally available materials to transform the most peaceable-looking rural settlement into a natural fortress. A deep, wide trench, sometimes serving as irrigation canal, surrounds the hamlet. The excavated dirt becomes a protective rampart from behind which men can safely fire their weapons. Everywhere there are narrow slit trenches and spider holes where men can hide. For shelter, every family builds a bunker of dry clay right under its bed, which is a thick board of hard wood. Big earthen jars are buried in the ground to serve as air-raid shelters for the young children.

Under the hamlet are tunnels dug by women and children, their secret entrances hidden under thickets of bamboo or between the roots of banana trees. Recesses in the walls hold ammunition and food. In an emergency, or if the village becomes occupied by American or South Vietnamese forces, its young men disappear into the maze of underground passages and remain hidden until the enemy has left. Some tunnels, as in the Cuchi district, twenty miles north of Saigon, are several hundred yards long and connect one combat hamlet with another. Twenty determined guerrillas resisting in a combat hamlet can keep a battalion of troops pinned down for several hours.

When weapons are not available, anything will do. On some occasions, mainly in the rugged highlands, the Vietcong urge villagers to raise venom-bearing wild bees. Their sting is painful and can send a soldier to the infirmary for some days. Poisonous snakes are also tried out in some regions to slow down American or Australian soldiers—but not Vietnamese, who catch and eat the reptiles, regarded as a delicacy in the Orient.

A man who has paid great attention to the building of combat hamlets and guerrilla bases is Lieutenant General Hoang Van Thai, former deputy chief of North Vietnam's People's Army. In August 1967, it was announced in Saigon that General Thai had succeeded Nguyen Chi Thanh as commander-in-chief of all Vietcong forces. Before assuming his new command, General Thai had something to say on the subject of fortified villages in the countryside:

"We must unceasingly consolidate and extend our guerrilla base areas and build combat villages. They constitute the rear as well as the fortresses of the guerrilla forces. In consequence, the launching and maintenance of guerrilla warfare are closely connected with the consolidation and extension of guerrilla bases and with the building of combat villages.

"The primary condition in setting up a guerrilla base is the political consciousness of the masses of the people. Therefore, to build solid guerrilla bases and combat villages, leading cadres and guerrilla forces must stick to the people and to the place where they operate. They must constantly educate, organize, and lead the masses to the struggle; see to it that the masses' living conditions be improved; distribute land to the peasants if local conditions permit.

"We must take advantage of the facilities of the terrain or modify it to make it suit our purpose: erect simple yet efficient defense works, underground hiding-places, spike and other traps, mine fields, to check the enemy's mopping-up operations, and preserve our bases. We must not only constantly consolidate the combat hamlets politically, militarily, and economically, but also enlarge them by upgrading and transforming guerrilla zones into guerrilla bases. We must create as many of these as possible to establish a system of bases supporting one another to encircle and scatter enemy troops, and thus better strike at them."

Next to the village, on Vietcong organization charts, is the district. Roughly the equivalent of an American county, a district includes four to six villages, each a cluster of four to eight combat hamlets. In each district, a clandestine chapter of the Lao Dong Party provides political leadership to the guerrilla movement. Its trusted members are drawn from the three-man cells existing in almost every hamlet and village. If liaison with the party's higher echelons is destroyed, the district chapter should be able to carry on the party's plan for six months, or even longer.

Decisions reached in secret meetings of party chapters (perhaps twelve members) are passed on to party cells in villages, which, in turn, brief the members of the various associations in the village. If the decision is military, the "command committee" of the village guerrilla unit is informed. If the decision is political, the Revolutionary Youth Group is mobilized jointly with the Liberation Farmers Association to implement the plan. It might be an order to prepare food rations for a Vietcong battalion that will shortly visit the village, or to ready canoes to ferry a guerrilla unit across a river. All militia and guerrilla forces in hamlets and villages are under the command of the local party chapter. At all levels of the guerrilla organization, political cadres are placed in command.

Everywhere, from top to bottom, orders and instructions flow down the party's invisible chain of command until they reach the last remote hamlet. District chapters receive their own instructions from thirty-three provincial party chapters (Vietcong provinces do not always correspond to the geographical boundaries of Vietnamese provinces). In turn, the provinces receive their guidance from seven zones, one of which deals exclusively with the Saigon metropolitan area. At the apex of the system is the Current Affairs Section of the Central Office for South Vietnam (COSVN). A recently captured Vietcong document says that this political organization should be preferred to the former "government-style administration" set up by the administrative councils that some Vietcong villages elected on their own initiative. Significantly, the same document urged lower party echelons to develop initiative, "but avoid independently changing the basic substance of requirements, tasks, and methods set forth by COSVN."

So much for the complex, political infrastructure of the movement. Because it is so deeply rooted among the peasantry and so well prepared for clandestine work, it takes much exhausting effort for a Vietnamese province chief to eliminate the enemy's party organization in his area.

Parallel to party chapters in districts and provinces are guerrilla units operating within these geographical limits. Each Vietcong province fields its own regional battalion, whose strength may vary from 300 to 600 men. Some of the provincial units, such as the famous Phu Loi Battalion of Thudaumot Province, northeast of Saigon, are as good as any regular unit coming from North Vietnam. The Phu Loi has an advantage: Recruited from the area, its men know the local geography better than anyone else.

Vietcong leaders give close attention to coordinating actions between regular units—organized in battalions, regiments, and even divisions—and the paramilitary forces, expecially between provincial battalions and the militias in villages and combat hamlets. General Hoang Van Thai—who, like Vo Nguyen Giap, started out as a schoolteacher in North Vietnam—has this to say on military coordination among guerrilla units:

"The militia constitutes the paramilitary force of the masses—first of all, of the toiling peasants. Militias do not give up production, they carry it on, and while embarking in production they fight to safeguard it, they stick to the people and to their locality, forming the core of guerrilla forces in villages.

"Local troops are the armed forces of provinces and districts, the core of the guerrilla forces there and the link between the militia and regular troops. While the people's militia conducts the struggle in villages, pinning down the enemy and creating conditions for local troops to muster and destroy him, the local forces assume the heavy task of helping the militia to develop. On the other hand, when regular troops scatter in small units to start guerrilla warfare at the enemy's rear, their duty is to train the local troops and militia. Close coordination between the military and paramilitary forces is a condition to ensure the growth of guerrilla warfare into regular warfare."

At present, the Vietcong is trying to raise its village guerrilla force from 160,000 to 200,000 or 250,000 men, with difficulty it seems—except perhaps in the densely populated Mekong delta. The reason for this forceful recruitment drive is easy to understand. According to Vietcong strategic plans, the guerrilla force should be strong enough to compel the enemy (primarily the Saigon government and the United States,) to distract 60 to 70 percent of its forces to protect its rear and cities against guerrilla harassments. During the Indochinese war in North Vietnam the Vietminh achieved that result, and the French, increasingly drawn to a defensive stand, were ultimately defeated. This is the balance of force that the Vietcong is trying to achieve in South Vietnam.

A striking illustration of this strategy is found in the Mekong delta, the "forgotten front" of the Vietnamese war. With 6,000,000 inhabitants, the flat, soggy delta is South Vietnam's most densely populated region and produces most of its food.

For military purposes, the Vietcong has two major commands in the delta: Zone 3, which roughly corresponds to the newly developed provinces west of the Mekong River; and Zone 2, including all the provinces between the Mekong and Saigon. According to U.S. statistics, the Vietcong controls 70 percent of the delta's land area and 50 percent of its population. Vietcong influence ranges from almost nil in the Hoa Hao Buddhist province of Angiang to 90 percent in Anxuyen, at the tip of the Camau Peninsula.

To keep main roads and canals open to traffic and to garrison the provincial cities, the Vietnamese army maintains 200,000 men in the delta, including 44 battalions of regulars.

192 AGE OF THE GUERRILLA

192 AGE OF THE GUERRILLA

Despite this huge force, progress is admittedly slow, and the situation is stagnating.

Facing them are 80,000 armed Vietcong. Some 60,000 of these are village and district guerrillas constituting the Vietcong home guard. The others, about 20,000 men, are organized in provincial battalions and main-force units. They do most of the heavy fighting against ARVN regulars and United States troops. Vietcong main-force battalions operate independently or carry out occasional regiment-size attacks against larger objectives. According to United States intelligence officers, the Vietcong "order of battle" in the delta lists 70 district companies of 80 to 120 men each; 11 provincial battalions of about 500 men each; 12 main-force battalions which can form four regiments. The Vietcong strategy in the delta is less the capture of major towns than the ceaseless harassment of government positions, so that no troops can be wthdrawn from the area for other fronts.

Early in 1967, as several Vietcong battalions made a threatening pincer movement against Route 4, the delta's main commercial artery with Saigon, General Westmoreland moved one 3,000-man brigade of the United States 9th Infantry Division into the area to operate as a riverine force. While the pressure on Route 4 was eased, pacification of the countryside made little progress, mainly because the Vietnamese battalions were unable to root out the Vietcong infrastructure from the villages.

U.S. STRATEGY IN VIETNAM

"American warfare in Vietnam is primarily helicopter warfare . . ."

General Moshe Dayan

In August 1964, General William C. Westmoreland assumed command of the United States war effort in South Vietnam; and several months later, following a series of bitter setbacks suffered by the Vietnamese army, planned the buildup that gradually brought the number of United States and other non-Vietnamese troops in Vietnam over the 500,000 mark. Simultaneously, the South Vietnamese armed forces were increased to 719,238, including a combat strength of 220,000 regulars, the rest being paramilitary and police troops.

As Westmoreland saw it, he inherited in Vietnam very few physical assets on which to build and develop a sophisticated military establishment. The first American troops to land in the country provided security for the three important airfields of Danang, Bienhoa, and Vungtau, since airpower was to play a crucial role in United States military doctrine. In all, 1,000 combat aircraft were deployed in Southeast Asia.

Westmoreland's next step was to develop a physical infrastructure of ports, communications, and logistical facilities through which he could support a rapidly expanding field force. This was the construction phase of the military buildup: Camranh Bay, Quinhon, Chulai were developed as deep-draft ports. Then, Westmoreland pushed inland, with the 1st Air Cavalry Division setting up its tents on the plateau of Ankhe, and the 25th U.S. Infantry Division securing Pleiku, the main jet airfield in the highlands.

By the summer of 1965, General Westmoreland had received enough troops to broaden the perimeter of security around Saigon and to reopen sections of vital Highway 1 in Central Vietnam, from Camranh Bay to Quinhon. The sea-girt enclaves of Chulai and Danang were expanded. Meanwhile, a new threat from the North compelled Westmoreland to deploy the 3rd Marine Division along the Demilitarized Zone (DMZ), to develop Phubai and Dongha as new forward bases, and to reinforce the garrison of Khesanh to block a likely invasion route across the mountains from Laos. The center of gravity of the war began to shift north, away from the Mekong delta, which, five years earlier, had been the cradle of the guerrilla forces.

One interesting footnote to the buildup: In the absence of any well-defined counterinsurgency doctrine, the United States Army disregarded the previous experience of its own Special Forces in Vietnam. The Army decided to fight the guerrillas with conventional forces, including a heavy reliance on artillery fire, air power, and even armor. The only tactical innovation was to give added mobility to United States ground troops by providing them with some 2,000 helicopters, the true flying workhorses of the Vietnamese war. Such a force required heavy logistics. The war became increasingly expensive.

By that time, United States officials in Vietnam began to say that there were "forty-four different wars in Vietnam, one going on independently in each province." The fact is that unlike Korea, here no linear front could be established: The war was made up of countless engagements flaring unexpectedly in the most unlikely places; one day along the desertlike coast, and the next deep in the virgin teak forests near the Laotian border.

This type of war was becoming a puzzle for United States operations officers trained to move divisions in a less disorderly manner. In fact, the United States 25th Infantry Division had two brigades fighting in the rice paddies on the periphery of Saigon, while its other brigade—airlifted straight from Hawaii—was 250 miles away, watching the Cambodian border. A similar situation later developed in the 4th Infantry Division, whose three brigades were engaged on three different fronts, hundreds of miles apart. Things were eventually straightened out when the two divisions traded brigades—the 25th was concentrated in the South and the 4th in Central Vietnam.

Early in 1966, General Westmoreland dispatched the 101st Airborne Brigade to secure the population and the rice crop in the coastal province of Phuyen, where South Vietnamese forces were gradually losing control of the area to the 3rd Vietcong Division. In the South, the 1st Infantry Division was reopening Route 13, the commercial link between Saigon and the rubber-producing country north of the Vietnamese capital. West of Saigon, the 25th Division (Tropic Lighting) was moving into the guerrilla-infested rice fields of Haunghia Province, where South Vietnamese army battalions were being trounced one after another by the Vietcong.

As Westmoreland began to get the necessary wherewithal for his mission—men, firepower, and logistical support—his strategy began to take shape: to let the enemy hold the foodless jungles and destroy him when he started to concentrate his forces to move toward the valleys near the coast. But it takes more than tactical ingenuity to move troops in the primitive environment of a Southeast Asian country. And Westmoreland had to wait until his supplies could flow smoothly through nine ocean harbors and eight jet airports. In addition, his engineers opened 68 smaller airfields throughout the country; from any one of them a full 5,000-man brigade of troops could be airlifted in a matter of hours. All this provided him with operational flexibility. Regardless of the scarcity of roads, or their destruction by the enemy, the general could move his troops about.

By early 1967, Westmoreland had enough infantry and armored battalions to accelerate the tempo of spoiling operations against 14 of the 41 known Vietcong bases, most of them within 50 miles of Saigon. His forces consumed a monthly average of 1,000,000 rounds of artillery and 700,000 mortar rounds plus 100,000,000 small arms rounds, a truly fantastic rate of consumption, an apocalyptic power of destruction to be used on a relatively weak enemy. High-flying B-52 bombers began saturation bombing of suspected areas of enemy concentrations.

A totally different war from either World War II or Korea, Vietnam calls for different types of military operations by ground troops. The major ones, as defined by General Westmoreland, and followed by General Abrams, have been:

1) Search-and-destroy operations, designed to seek out Vietcong bases and destroy their supplies, communications, and installations. Also called "spoiling operations," these actions are not designed to seize and hold territory permanently. Most of the time, they take place in jungle areas where the guerrillas have set up secret bases.

2) Clear-and-secure operations to eliminate residual Vietcong forces permanently from specified limited areas. These operations can last as long as a year and are designed to hold populated territory and prevent the return of the guerrillas. They are also called "operations of pacification."

3) Reserve-reaction operations, designed to relieve provincial capitals and district towns under Vietcong attack and to quickly reinforce, when needed, friendly units engaged by larger enemy forces. The operations in Locninh and Dakto in November 1967 were reserve-reaction operations.

4) Defense of government centers, including the protection of provincial capitals, district towns, and key facilities and installations such as airbases and ports. Except in Central Vietnam, where the United States Marines provide protection to airbases and bridges, static defense is essentially carried out by South Vietnamese forces. It sometimes requires extensive patrolling to prevent the enemy from setting up mortars and rockets on the periphery of the installations.

5) Missions of surveillance, carried out by U.S. and South Vietnamese Special Forces and Civilian Irregulars (CIDG) along the land frontiers of South Vietnam. Their mission is to detect enemy infiltration and buildup of troops in frontier areas rarely visited by friendly ground forces.

A MASSIVE ONSLAUGHT
AGAINST THE HEADQUARTERS
OF THE VIETNAM GUERRILLAS

Day after day, the great, lumbering B-52s flew high over-head, dropping ton after ton of explosives on the tangled jungle fastness near the Cambodian border known as War Zone C. Then, one morning, after swarms of low-flying jets had softened up the zone even further with rockets and ma-chine-gun fire, the assault began. Wave after wave of heli-copters fluttered in over the treetops, landing and disgorg-ing thousands of United States infantrymen. In the very middle of the zone, the sky was suddenly alive with para-troopers, floating gracefully to earth in the first U.S. combat jump of the Vietnamese war. And from the outskirts of Zone C, along the roads and through the underbrush, thousands more United States and South Vietnamese ground troops closed in.

"Operation Junction City," the biggest United States mili-tary offensive of the Vietnamese war, was under way. In-volving more than 30,000 men under the overall command of Lieutenant General Jonathan Seaman, Junction City was designed to close a trap on an estimated 10,000 elite guer-rillas said to be in the area. More important yet, there was the hope of bagging the leadership of the Vietcong, whose headquarters was hidden deep in the forests of Zone C, the rarely visited bastion of the Vietnamese insurgents.

The field headquarters of the Vietnamese guerrillas has

198 AGE OF THE GUERRILLA

the title of Central Office for South Vietnam (COSVN). This strategic site was, at the time, located in the northern part of Tayninh Province, a mere 70 miles northwest of Saigon. From there, the leaders of COSVN have easy access to neutral Cambodia, where they can take refuge in case of serious military difficulties. The Cambodian sanctuary also offers them rapid communications and liaison with Hanoi. Without such a convenient sanctuary, it is doubtful whether the South Vietnamese insurgency would be able to survive. At least, it would experience more serious problems.

Before launching Operation Junction City, U.S. intelligence had obtained a considerable wealth of information about the ranking members of COSVN. A four-star general in the North Vietnamese army, General Nguyen Chi Thanh, was military commander of the Vietcong forces. Thanh was believed to have arrived in South Vietnam toward the end of 1964, as Hanoi made the crucial decision to send the first organized North Vietnamese army unit—then a regiment—to the South. Through the months, 50,000 to 60,000 North Vietnamese soldiers eventually followed to reinforce the "Liberation Front Armed Forces." In fact, Nguyen Chi Thanh may have been killed during Operation Junction City—perhaps caught in his underground shelter by a B-52 bombardment. Some time later, Hanoi officially announced Thanh's death "of a heart attack." Thanh was only in his late forties, and pictures of him captured in South Vietnam showed a healthy man, sitting on a hammock in the forest of War Zone C. Like other top-ranking Vietcong leaders, Thanh had bodyguards who would never have allowed him to be captured alive by his enemies.

General Thanh's deputies in COSVN were two other North Vienamese army generals, both alternate members of the Lao Dong (Workers) Party Central Committee, the elite political body of North Vietnam. Lieutenant General Tran Van Tra, a deputy chief of staff of the North Vietnamese army, served, and presumably still does, as Deputy Commander of the "Liberation Armed Forces," the standing army of the Vietcong, and had been in South Vietnam since 1960 or 1961. Major General Tran Do, a tough, husky Vietnamese, served as Deputy Political Officer of the Liberation Forces. These three Hanoi-trained generals were regarded as the military brains of the Vietcong; they knew the art of guerrilla warfare superbly well both as tacticians and strategists. To capture or kill them was the American goal for Operation Junction City. Of course, U.S. soldiers would also have been happy to get their hands on lawyer Nguyen Huu Tho, the head of the National Liberation Front, the political arm of the Vietcong.

Thus the background and purpose of Junction City was a search-and-destroy operation, a monumental and dangerous manhunt that continued for more than eight weeks through silent Buddhist monasteries and dark jungles. I joined a platoon of the U.S. 1st Infantry Division (known to military men as the Big Red One) on the first day of the action.

The platoon was badly undermanned and critically short of noncoms. Some of the men, who were carrying sausagelike links of green woolen socks stuffed with cans of beer tied to their belts, made a strangely unmilitary appearance. But the platoon seemed to be well led by First Lieutenant David Cejka.

As we followed a dirt trail leading toward Cambodia, an unnaturally loud-voiced cuckoo began to sing. By experience, I knew it was not a bird, but I kept my mouth shut. These men did not need any advice, I thought, and I was right. "I can smell Charlies all around us," said one young

sergeant. (Charlie is the Americans' nickname for the Vietcong.)

For a while we plodded ahead through paddies and
hedgerows of cactus and tangled bamboo. My eyes were on
the ground, looking for telltale signs of mines or booby
traps. Then, as we entered a bamboo thicket, there came a
hail of automatic weapons fire. Suddenly the tall platoon
sergeant and some other men fell and lay still on the ground
like disjointed dolls.

The last thing to do in a situation like this is stay put and
let fear take command. Lieutenant Cejka realized this and
quickly rallied his men. "Charge! Charge!" he shouted, and
his men crashed forward 30 yards through the bamboo, firing as they went. Our small counterattack achieved its purpose. For the time being, the attackers had been thrown
back. It was at this point that I began to keep notes.
The hardly legible scrawling in my notebook reads:

11 A.M. The Vietcong are hiding somewhere, just yards
away. I know that I have to keep busy snapping pictures and
taking notes. Otherwise I'll start worrying about the bullets
that occasionally whine out of the bamboo. Giant red ants
fall from the trees onto our necks; and their sting can drive
a man mad. The soldiers have taped small plastic bottles of
insect repellent on their steel helmets. I don't even carry a
helmet.

11:30: Enemy fire comes from two directions, and it looks
as though they're trying to outflank us. Lieutenant Cejka orders the two platoon medics to recover the men wounded
in the first attack. "Put some covering fire in front of them!"
the lieutenant shouts to his machine gunners. The medics
crawl, run, crawl, and run again, then disappear. They don't
wear helmets or carry weapons; that would slow them
down.

11:45: In the distance, we can make out B-57 bombers striking a target. Some other unit must be in trouble. But why don't we get any air or artillery support? In Saigon they tell us that it takes only fifteen minutes to bring in an air strike. We have been pinned down for forty-five minutes, and still no help. The artillerymen are certainly less than 2 miles away. Why aren't they firing?

11:50: The medics have dragged in four wounded men who cannot walk or crawl and have to be carried. The two medics are superb. Now they are giving morphine shots, water, and cigarettes to the wounded.

12:00: "Throw up a smoke grenade!" yells Lieutenant Cejka. "The dust-off (medical evacuation helicopter) is coming." The wounded are soon loaded aboard, the copter takes off quickly as shots ring out from the nearby woods.

12:10: Now, at last, some air cover. Overhead, the observation planes have marked the enemy's position with a white phosphorus rocket. And here comes the artillery, protecting our right flank with a barrage of 105-mm. shells. An error of a few yards, and the whole platoon would be wiped out.

12:15: Helicopters are spraying the nearby bush with their rapid-firing machine guns. Other choppers called "hogs" spit hissing rockets around the landscape. Lieutenant Cejka gives them directions by radio. Meanwhile, the invisible guerrillas continue to harass us with short bursts of AK-47 sub-machine guns.

12:30: The jets are here. First, the dart-shaped Super Sabres zoom in at treetop level, so close and so fast that we can feel their warm exhaust. They unload their pointed fragmentation bombs, and the precision is amazing. Between passes of the screaming jets, I swear I can hear high-pitched North Vietnamese voices behind us. Some of them seem to come from the ground. Are we on top of a tunnel system? I keep staring around, but minutes later the talking has faded away. This war is full of surprises.

12:35: The F-100's are relieved by a flight of four B-57 Canberra jets, which drop their eggs of napalm just ahead of us. Sometimes a napalm bomb comes uncomfortably close. "Hit the dirt!" yells Cejka, and no one is hurt. If you stay on your belly, you are pretty safe. The cactus plants are splashed with big drops of napalm that failed to ignite. I pick up a sticky droplet. It smells like rubber cement and looks like shaving cream.

12:40: Two more wounded men and the dead platoon sergeant are brought in by the medics. A green poncho is pulled over the dead man, the wounded are bandaged. One of them is in bad shape. By radio, Lieutenant Cejka gets word that the remnant of his platoon is to link up with another unit for the rest of the sweep. But I have seen enough fighting for the day, and I am glad to be lifted out with the casualties. The badly wounded man, who may have only minutes to live, bleeds silently and profusely. His dark blood drips onto my boots. Gently, I help the medic wrap him in a green army blanket.

The object of Operation Junction City was to disrupt what the United States command thought was a well-established guerrilla base. Initially, during the first ten days of the operation, the major enemy units reported in the area did not react significantly, and the only encounters were against a thin screen of guerrillas left behind to slow down the three-pronged U.S. thrust. Then the three main-force regiments of the 9th Vietcong Division launched four separate counterattacks against the defensive perimeters of American units. Invariably, the enemy tried to swamp the Americans in close fighting before the Air Force could intervene massively. No matter how sophisticated the coordination between ground troops and the Air Force, it is difficult to obtain air support in less than twenty minutes, and the Vietcong knows it.

The fiercest engagement took place on April 1, more than a month after the start of the operation on February 22. A large Vietcong force, estimated at regiment strength, attacked the headquarters of the United States 2nd Brigade and the bivouac of two American infantry battalions at Apgu, a forest clearing twenty-five miles northeast of the provincial capital of Tayninh. The battle raged from dawn into the morning. After heavy mortar attacks on the American positions, the guerrillas launched human-wave assaults, penetrating the American defense perimeter. The Vietcong made desperate efforts to reinforce the small element of troops that had managed to break through the United States lines. This group had a machine gun, but it was knocked out later during the battle by an extremely accurate air strike carried out by American fighter bombers. After the engagement, the 2nd Infantry Brigade claimed the enemy had left 609 dead guerrillas in front of its lines.

In four engagements, United States troops killed 925 guerrillas, captured only nine with twelve weapons: mortars and machine guns. Although the COSVN leaders evacuated their headquarters to another location as American troops approached, they left behind a wealth of documents— some 202 pounds worth, including detailed guidance from Hanoi. COSVN provides the direct link between the southern guerrilla movement and North Vietnam. One particularly significant document was the tape of an address by North Vietnamese General Nguyen Van Vinh, chairman of the Lao Dong Party's Reunification Department. General Vinh, who is also a deputy chief of staff, traveled from Hanoi to COSVN headquarters, a trip of some 800 miles, in April 1966, to deliver his instructions in person to the guerrilla leaders. He was extremely confident about the Vietcong's chances to wear out and ultimately defeat the American troops within "four or five years."

Searching the forests and deserted villages of War Zone C, American paratroopers uncovered the clandestine radio station of the Liberation Front and a recording studio; its transmitters, however, had been removed. Typically, the building, totally invisible from above, had 1-foot-thick walls filled with sand, insulated doors, and even double glass windows. It was as soundproof as any American radio studio. Twenty base camps used as training schools by the guerrillas were also uncovered. One contained a medical center with large quantities of medical supplies, another a printing shop. Each had its own set of field kitchens, half buried in the ground and nearly smokeless.

The kitchens were laid out in such a way that the source of heat would not register on the infrared cameras of United States observation aircraft. Infrared photography—known as Red Haze—is extensively practiced in South Vietnam for detecting the camps of guerrillas beneath the jungle. Obviously, the guerrillas have learned to cope with this problem, as with many others. In all, United States troops destroyed 1,140 bunkers, 384 shelters, and 59 underground tunnels that were part of the installations built by the guerrillas.

Eventually, American and South Vietnamese troops pulled out from War Zone C, and the guerrillas moved in again. This was in April. By fall, after an uneventful rainy season, the leadership of the guerrillas had recovered from the disruption of their organization by Operation Junction City. The 7th NVA division came down from its staging area in southern Laos and moved into War Zone C to provide protection to the central organs of the insurgency. Meanwhile, Division 9 quietly slipped out of the area and made a move toward War Zone D, 50 miles to the east, where the U.S. 1st Division vainly tried to pursue it. But this was only a feint. By October, the three regiments of Division 9 were back to full strength after receiving replacement personnel and new weapons from the North. On November 1 they carried out a sustained assault against the administrative center and the Special Forces camp at Locninh, near the Cambodian border. It thus became clear that the resilient guerrillas had recovered from the effects of Operation Junction City. They were ready for another offensive, this time on a new front of their choice.

GUERRILLA WARFARE IN A BIG CITY:
THE BATTLE FOR SAIGON

It was late on January 31, 1968, the first night of Tet, the Vietnamese lunar new year, and most of Saigon's 3,000,000 inhabitants were fast asleep, groggy after a day of feasting on squid and sugarcane and endless bottles of La Rue beer. Along broad, brightly lit Thong Nhut Boulevard, a slender man named Nguyen Van Muoi slowly guided his black Citroën sedan past a gleaming white building. In the back seat of the car, Muoi carried an elaborately carved samurai sword as a good-luck charm. Shortly before 3 A.M., as he approached the building once again, Muoi glanced at his watch and then shouted out of the car window. *"Tien!"* (Forward!) he yelled. *"Tien!"* And with that signal, nineteen young commandos—all members of the Vietcong's elite C-10 Sapper Battalion—surged from their hiding places in the shadows of trees and dashed down the street toward the United States Embassy.

Thus began a bold and bloody assault on the sprawling United States Embassy compound in the heart of downtown Saigon. As a thunderous barrage of mortars and rockets slammed into the sleeping capital, the nineteen terrorists swiftly went about their work. Two young U.S. Military Policemen standing guard by a side gate were gunned down in the first moments of the attack. Simultaneously, some of the raiders blew a gaping hole through the Embassy's outer wall with a 3.5-inch bazooka and clambered through it. The first to spot them was the Embassy's night-duty chauffeur. Unarmed, he rushed forward in an impulsive attempt to stop the intruders—and was instantly mowed down in a hail of fire from Chinese-made AK-47 sub-machine guns.

Once inside the Embassy garden, the lead commandos blew the lock off the side gate on Mac Dinh Chi Street and admitted their comrades. Then the full complement of heavily armed men—dressed in green slacks and shirts with red armbands—fanned out through the 4-acre compound. Within seconds, each man was crouching at the precise position that he had been taught to take during long and arduous months of secret training for the attack.

Inside the main chancellery building, two American civilians—trapped in the communications and code rooms on the fourth floor—reported by telephone that the Embassy was under siege. Shortly thereafter, the phone lines were cut. Downstairs, two Marine guards ran across the floodlit marble floor of the lobby toward the teakwood doors at the front entrance.

By now, the alarm had been sounded throughout Saigon. Four blocks away, United States Ambassador Ellsworth Bunker was whisked from his residence beside the city's old European cemetery to a secret security dwelling set up for such an emergency. And not quite twenty minutes after the attack began, a "reaction force" of six MP's from the 716th Police Battalion arrived outside the Embassy—only to be pinned down in the gutters by enemy fire. Two more MP's, careening around a corner in a jeep, drove directly into the blistering crossfire and were killed. From then on, throughout the night, the terrorists fought back from behind the Embassy's man-sized flowerpots and massive pillars.

With first light, Army Major Hillel Schwartz, who had only recently arrived in Vietnam, received orders over his field radio to lead his first helicopter assault of the war—against his own Embassy. Twice, the "Huey" helicopters carrying Schwartz and two platoons of "Screaming Eagle" paratroopers from the 101st Airborne Division fluttered within yards of the Embassy's rooftop landing pad—and twice they were driven off by a fusillade of heavy fire directed by the Vietcong from their entrenched positions.

Finally, a few minutes past 8 A.M., the small force of MP's in front of the Embassy charged directly into the enemy's line of fire. At 9 A.M., the last surviving guerrilla was killed in the lobby of the Embassy. American bureaucrats returned to their desks.

Thus, six full hours after the Vietcong first launched their attack, the U.S. Embassy compound was wrested back from their control. During the battle, five U.S. servicemen lost their lives and all nineteen of the terrorists were slain. To underscore the fact that the United States was once again master of its own diplomatic domain, Ambassador Bunker returned to the Embassy two hours after the fighting ended.

As late as Thursday night in Saigon, police stations in the crowded 6th, 7th and 8th precincts were coming under attack by well-organized Vietcong companies. In the 5th Precinct, the warren of narrow streets near the racetrack was alive with armed Communist propaganda teams equipped with bullhorns. Spouted the Vietcong propagandists: "This is total revolution. We are masters of the city. We ask you to join us." In some cases, these exhortations seemed to work. In the Phulam district, for example, 200 marchers defiantly paraded down the street carrying the blue-and-red National Liberation Front flag.

In some areas of the city, the guerrillas were seen entering private homes to drink tea with the residents and wish them a happy new year on behalf of the National Liberation Front. But the Vietcong cadres had not come simply to exchange pleasantries. They ordered the people to destroy their red-and-yellow South Vietnamese flags—and those who refused to do so were taken to the street and shot on the spot.

In the grim, charnel-house atmosphere, acts of calculated cruelty were all too common. When a youthful United States Army adviser stumbled by mistake into a street occupied by the Vietcong, he was captured, "tried," and publicly executed within a matter of minutes. A Vietnamese major, who had led an armored unit in the street fighting, returned home to find that his wife and children had been murdered by the enemy.

The government forces were quick to spill blood, too. During a bitter fight near An Quang pagoda, a manacled Vietcong suspect was brought to Gen. Nguyen Ngoc Loan, the National Police Chief who had taken personal charge of the pagoda operation. Dressed in civilian clothes, the young prisoner was wearing an armband stamped with the letters "X 2 B 27"—possibly a coded identification for "Cell Two, Platoon 27."

Unable to make the suspect talk, Loan took out his revolver, calmly pointed it at the prisoner's head, and shot him dead.

The Tet attack on Saigon was arrogantly conceived and boldly brought off. It carried the mark of a man well known to Western intelligence agencies and still at large: a veteran guerrilla leader named Nguyen Van Kham, better known to his associates as To Ky. In his late forties, To Ky acquired his first experience in guerrilla war in 1945 when he joined the anti-French resistance. As a member of the Dang Cong San (Communist Party) he became a skilled organizer of secret political units. (One mistake in his earlier youth gave the French Sûreté a chance to nab him. After several years in a French penitentiary, he resumed his political activities.)

By 1950, To Ky had a battalion of guerrillas under his command. French officers who fought him, always in the vicinity of Saigon, developed a grudging admiration for his ruthless tactics and his astonishing ability to survive. "To Ky is a worthy enemy," one of them admitted; "he is a master guerrilla." Born in South Vietnam, To Ky has Chinese blood, which renders him indistinguishable from the half-million Chinese traders who live in Saigon. Ironically, To Ky ended the Indochinese war as a full-fledged colonel in General Vo Nguyen Giap's People's Liberation Army and sat down with French officers to arrange the reassignment of Vietminh forces to North Vietnam after the 1954 Geneva agreements. The meeting, at Xuyenmoc, a Vietminh stronghold east of Saigon, was reasonably cordial. To Ky, like his French counterparts, had had enough of fighting and felt relieved by the end of the Indochinese war. But was it the end?

The reactivation of the Vietnamese war in 1959, this time between the supporters of Ho Chi Minh and the U.S. puppet government of President Ngo Dinh Diem, saw To Ky returning to his old hunting grounds in the South. Sometime in 1966, General To Ky took command of the newly created Capital Liberation Regiment, known also as Rgt. 165-A.

Unit 165-A was formed in 1966, when the National Liberation Front began to think seriously about an offensive against the South Vietnamese capital. Today it includes eight battalions, of fewer than 200 men each, positioned in the five suburban districts surrounding Saigon: Hocmon, Govap, Thuduc, Nhabe, and Binhchanh. Its arsenal includes automatic weapons, antitank rockets, and mortars. On D-Day, set for January 31, 1968, To Ky engaged only one battalion against Saigon while the others carried out multipronged attacks against military installations on the periphery.

There was plenty of warning. So much warning, in fact, that the only way to achieve surprise was for the Vietcong to exploit the usual Tet celebrations, all the attendant noise and festive paralysis of the city. Smuggling arms in was not difficult. A Vietnamese policeman assigned to check trucks coming into the city might wave through a shipment of vegetables for a 1,000-piaster bribe to supplement his modest monthly pay. But under the vegetables were several dozen AK-47's, B-40 rocket launchers (equivalent of a bazooka— in effect, a rocket-propelled, armor-piercing missile), and clips of ammunition.

There were many phony burial ceremonies; coffinloads of weapons were lowered into shallow graves where they could be dug up quickly. Vietcong agents also noticed that the police never seemed to visit unfinished building sites. Many construction workers were actually members of the Vietcong infrastructure, and an occasional bag of cement would contain weapons to be stored in the basement or on the uppermost level of a construction project. Hundreds of guerrillas rode into town openly on scooters, in pedicabs, and

in one case in a bus loaded with flowerpots. Under the
blooming cargo lay lethal weapons.

At Tet time it is virtually impossible for the police to search
anyone. Everyone in Saigon is celebrating the Lunar New
Year, and the police try not to disturb the public. If a policeman tried to search a three-wheeled Lambretta taxi on the
outskirts of the bustling city, crowds would quickly gather
and send him packing.

Four days before Tet, Colonel Nguyen Van Luan, the ur-
bane, 41-year-old head of the 17,000-man Saigon police,
was informed that two score brand-new AK-47 assault rifles had been found in one week. He had a vague premoni-
tion that something might happen on the first night of Tet.
As Luan was preparing to leave his office at 10:25 P.M., the
short-wave radio telephone crackled that a man had been
arrested with a burlap sack containing four AK-47's. Luan
decided to stay on, and sat down to a game of Chinese chess
with another officer on night duty. By 3 A.M., he decided
that nothing would happen that night. A few minutes later,
every radio at police headquarters came alive.

Most prisoners have now talked, and it is not hard to re-
construct the overall strategic plan and the tactical objectives of the guerrillas in Saigon. The strategic objective was
a pincer movement from north and south to sever the
district of Cholon from Saigon. The pincer's spearheads
were, from the north, the 6th Battalion of the 165-A regiment (Capital Liberation Regiment) and from the south
and west the 111th Regiment, formed in the prior six months
from several autonomous Vietcong companies marshaled in
the Mekong delta.

The 6th Battalion infiltrated the city from the direction
of Tansonnhut airport. One company was assigned to liberate the Chihoa Central Prison, where some 5,000 to 7,000

inmates were held; the Vietcong infrastucture was to take
the prisoners over, arm them, and get them to join the insurrection. The tactical missions of the 6th Battalion and
111th Regiment were quite independent of the suicide missions of commando squads that attacked the U.S. Embassy,
the Presidential Palace, the radio station, and four police
headquarters.

The 6th Battalion never reached Chihoa. It was stopped
by the police—who bore the brunt of the fighting, along
with U.S. MP's, for the first six hours—on the border of the
5th and 6th precincts near the Phutho racetrack. One prisoner said the "Big Chief" would rendezvous at the prison
after it was taken (perhaps Vietcong General Tran Do, who
was apparently in command of the Saigon operation). Another said they lost their guide early in the fighting. Such
mishaps plagued several battalions of peasant guerrillas,
who lost their way in the big, sprawling city.

The 111th Regiment didn't even do as well as the 6th Battalion. But its mission was harder; the terrain was flat, with
waterways to cross, and an early alarm was set off by the police. There, too, the field police fought desperately. One of
the principal objectives on that side of the town was the
Tanthuan bridge in the 4th Precinct, which would have
sealed off the port area. Something still unexplained went
wrong in that area, and the guerrilla group assigned to this
key objective failed to infiltrate the city.

Valid identity papers and voting registration cards were
later found on the bodies of several dead guerrillas. The Tet
firecrackers also played a key role in the infiltration. Ameri-
can-made firecrackers used in Vietnamese army training
camps to simulate combat conditions are hard to distinguish
from the noise of automatic weapons. They were for sale
in many Cholon stores; they provided a perfect noise cover
in the crucial initial stages of the attacks.

There was also police collusion on the periphery of the city, where the guerrillas were not detected until they were well inside. Some policemen simply made sure they would not be where they were supposed to be when the Vietcong attacked. But on the whole the police fought well when they came under attack. They suffered 80 dead and some 200 wounded.

If the Communists had decided to move a day earlier (as they did in Central Vietnam), they might have pulled it off. They would have had tens of thousands of Saigonese on the streets, returning from late pagoda services and on their way to family banquets. Persuading people already in the streets to demonstrate would have been easier, and chances are that the police would have held their fire. And by the time a huge demonstration was under way with banners demanding "peace" and "U.S. go home," it might have been too late for ARVN and U.S. troops to intervene.

The Vietcong have always had a well-oiled infrastructure in the city. Bars and most hotels pay protection money. Pharmacies are assessed for a drug quota each month for medical supplies. Money, food, equipment, drugs, anything they need, can be collected from merchants and citizens in the cities. How much of the infrastructure has been uprooted is hard to judge. Many cells have been destroyed, but most of them seem to be lateral cells that lead investigators along horizontal tracks rather than up the pyramid of command.

To maintain security during their elaborate preparation for the furious punch at Saigon, the leaders used a system of "compartmentalization" or "horizontal organization." Many of the guerrillas who converged on Saigon came empty-handed like ordinary farmers on a visit to the capital. Some spent a full day reconnoitering their objectives. Others were assigned a rendezvous point, where they were taken in charge by guides, usually pedicab drivers who had infiltrated the city a long time ahead. If one man was caught at this point, or defected, police interrogators would have learned little from him other than the fact that his squad or company leader had told him to spend the holiday season in Saigon and join the crowds shooting off firecrackers.

Weapons and explosives that had been smuggled into the city by a totally separate organization remained in safe caches until the last moment. Usually the caches were located in places unsuspected by the police, such as Chinese graveyards, warehouses, or factories. Throughout the city, the organization in charge of logistics maintained a vast network of camouflaged armories, and no trouble was spared to make the cover perfect. The "logisticians" were not aware of the plans of those who would receive and use the weapons, and vice versa.

One of the operational unit's most active command posts was installed in a small café known as Pho Binh. Binh, a respectable-looking North Vietnamese refugee, was responsible for the northern section of the capital, which includes the giant Tansonnhut airbase. After the attack, Binh quietly returned to his stove where he was arrested days later, after suspicious neighbors denounced him. But to this day, the complex organization of logistics with all its arms caches has remained almost intact, as the police were never able to identify the mysterious Vietcong logisticians. Some say they are very wealthy and very respectable Chinese, or Vietnamese, businessmen; others think they might be Buddhist monks.

Most of the 6th Battalion was sacrificed in the attack. Its commander and one company commander were killed; another company commander and the battalion's political commissar were captured. Of the 900 guerrillas who actually entered the city limits, 369 were killed and 51 captured.

Captain Phan Quang Tan, the head of the 600-man Police Special Branch in Saigon, a tough veteran of many Vietcong hunts in the city, had to spend the first few days desk-bound; an American "adviser" had dropped a weapon in front of Tan just before Tet and the accidental shot came up through his desk and shattered Tan's right arm. So Tan was able to devote many hours to interrogation of prisoners. Some refused to say anything and were shot; others talked to save their lives.

For two days Captain Tan played cat-and-mouse with a junior Vietcong officer. He promised him his life for details of his mission. Over beer and cigarettes, the Vietcong talked about many things other than his mission. At the end of the second day, Tan said quietly that he was sorry that the officer had chosen the path of death, but there was left no alternative. The Vietcong then said, "I suppose you're going to take me out to one of your public executions." Tan replied, "Oh no, we don't do that any more." For the first time the Communist officer looked anxious. "Then what are you going to do?" "In a few days," Captain Tan said matter-of-factly, "we will put an announcement in the papers, and your family will read that you were hit by an American truck and killed in a banal traffic accident." The prisoner returned to his cell. Next day he asked to see Tan again. He talked himself out, disclosing his mission and several other items of interest. He simply could not face the idea of his family's hearing about his inglorious end. A hero's death he was prepared for; his family would treasure his legend. But not a traffic accident. Tan's psychology worked.

Many other prisoners did not fare so well. Some, whom U.S. intelligence officers would like to interrogate again for cross-checking with subsequent revelations, have simply disappeared.

One Vietcong said he would lead ARVN soldiers to an arms cache. Instead he led the troopers, who were unfamiliar with the city, on a wild-goose chase, including two circles round the same block, which presumably gave others watching from houses time to escape. He, too, sacrificed his life to save the rest of his group.

The guerrillas had conceived a bold, imaginative scheme to achieve victory within twenty-four hours. A small commando group was to capture Premier Nguyen Van Loc and take him to the Saigon radio station, where he would be forced to read a proclamation on behalf of his government ordering all Vietnamese police and military forces to cease the fighting against the guerrillas. Other broadcasts would have urged the populace to rise and march in the streets to demand the departure of American troops from South Vietnam. The installation of a coalition administration of neutralist and liberal intellectuals would have followed immediately.

Meantime, other guerrilla units were to capture Tansonnhut International Airport, where the top leaders of the insurrection would have landed after flying from their secret hideouts in Cambodia. But the Vietcong had committed at least one key error in their otherwise well-coordinated plan. They neglected to interdict a 38-mile stretch of rice paddies between Saigon and the U.S. 25th Infantry Division base at Trang Bang. This could have been done easily by positioning a blocking force on the northern flank of the city.

The oversight enabled the 3rd Squadron, 4th Cavalry, to knife its way to Saigon with forty armored vehicles, barreling down surprised guerrillas along the highway and even whipping through the town of Cuchi while the Vietcong still occupied it. At the outskirts of Saigon, the squadron immediately engaged—and helped throw back—500 Vietcong who had seized a foothold on the southwest runway of Tan-sonnhut airport. The guerrillas were unable to reinforce their men, who had already invaded the airport, and the attackers were crushed.

The Tet offensive ended March 1, leaving one hundred South Vietnamese cities bruised after crushing blows inflicted by nearly half a million guerrillas. A second round of widespread urban attack followed in May and June, as the guerrillas fired 122-mm. and 107-mm. rockets into cities at an average range of six miles. The rocket attacks demoralized the civilians, but due to poor accuracy, they were not effective against purely military targets.

One result of the rocket threat was to compel the United States and South Vietnamese commanders to protect the cities instead of pursuing the guerrillas.

Another effective weapon the guerrillas used in the period following Tet was the Russian-made RPG antitank launcher. Carried by an infantryman, it can penetrate 11 inches of steel. The RPG, known also as the BBB 40, claimed a high toll of United States armor and enabled the guerrillas to ambush mechanized columns.

The leaders of Tet had expected their offensive to spark a general uprising against the Saigon government. This it failed to do, but for six months it succeeded in keeping 1,200,000 allied troops on the defensive, and it gave the guerrilla movement the impetus of a strategic offensive, both militarily and politically. Eventually the United States and South Vietnamese recovered a measure of initiative, yet the psychological impact on American and world opinion was enough to convince the United States that, short of resorting to nuclear weapons, the prospect of a conventional military victory in Vietnam at an acceptable price and within an acceptable time frame was hopeless. It was this awareness that led President Johnson on March 31, 1968, to order a partial bombing halt of North Vietnam and to open diplomatic negotiations for a political settlement.

Intermittent rocketing of Vietnamese cities continued until October 31. Hours after the last rocket crashed on a Saigon church, killing 19 civilians, Johnson ordered the complete cessation of acts of war against North Vietnam. Despite a total loss of 1,000 warplanes over North Vietnam, the air war had never achieved its objective of limiting the infiltration of men and matériel into South Vietnam.

During the Tet and subsequent urban assaults, the NLF lost about 100,000 men—about one-fifth its armed manpower. Nowhere were the guerrillas able to hold a city they had overrun despite sacrifices of thousands of "ready-to-die" volunteers. The Tet offensive was a short-lived military success, yet it was an undeniable political victory. Guerrilla warfare had entered a new phase, and to meet it at a level that would cost $30,000,000,000 annually and at a loss of 10,000 American lives every year had become plainly unacceptable to the United States. Already mounting opposition to the war and to the draft had forced both the Republican and Democratic presidential candidates to take positions against the war.

DOCUMENTS

DOCUMENT 1

ASIAN BACKGROUNDS ESSAYS BY SUN TZU

ABOUT THE DOCUMENT

Sun Tzu's essays on "The Art of War" are the earliest known writings on the subject of guerrilla fighting. Written 2,500 years ago, they shed penetrating light on the Asiatic philosophy of war.

Sun Tzu believed that moral strength and intellectual capacity are decisive in war. His primary target was the mind of the opposing commander. He considered that war should be preceded by measures designed to make it easy to win, and that an indispensable preliminary was an attack on the mind of the enemy. In his view, the expert commander strikes only when the situation assures victory; to create such a situation is the ultimate responsibility of generalship. Basic to his thesis is that those deprived of the initiative usually lose.

Sun Tzu has been the bedrock on which most Asiatic writings on war are based. A thorough understanding of Sun Tzu will enable the modern observer to comprehend better the "war of liberation" as conducted by guerrillas throughout the world. The following are excerpts from the essays.

THE DOCUMENT

Strategy: Bewilder the enemy.

"To capture the enemy's army is better than to destroy it; to take intact a battalion, a company, or a five-man squad is better than to destroy them.

"When your weapons are dulled and ardor damped, your strength exhausted and treasure spent, neighboring rulers will take advantage of your distress to act. And even though you have wise counselors, none will be able to lay good plans for the future."

"To win one hundred victories in one hundred battles is not the acme of skill. To subdue the enemy without fighting is the acme of skill.

"Thus, what is of supreme importance in war is to attack the enemy's strategy.

"Next best is to disrupt his alliances.

"The next best is to attack his army.

"Thus a victorious army wins its victories before seeking battle; an army destined to defeat fights in the hope of winning.

"Know yourself, know your enemy."

"War is a matter of vital importance to the state; the province of life or death; the road to survival or ruin. It is mandatory that it be thoroughly studied.

"Therefore, appraise it in terms of the five fundamental factors. . . .

"The first of these factors is moral influence; the second, weather; the third, terrain; the fourth, command; the fifth, doctrine.

"By moral influence, I mean that which causes the people

to be in harmony with their leaders, so that they will accompany them in life and unto death without fear of mortal peril.

"By weather, I mean the interaction of natural forces; the effects of winter's cold and summer's heat and the conduct of military operations in accordance with the seasons.

"By terrain, I mean distances, whether the ground is traversed with ease or difficulty, whether it is open or constricted, and the chances of life or death.

"By command, I mean the general's qualities of wisdom, sincerity, humanity, courage, and strictness.

"By doctrine, I mean organization, control, assignment of appropriate ranks to officers, regulation of supply routes, and provision of principal items used by the army.

"There is no general who has not heard of these five matters. Those who master them win; those who do not are defeated."

Intelligence: The Divine Thread.

"Now there are five sorts of secret agents to be employed. These are native, inside, double, expendable, and living.

"When these five types of agents are all working simultaneously and none knows their method of operation, they are called "The Divine Thread" and are the treasure of a sovereign.

"Native agents are those of the enemy's people whom we employ.

"Inside agents are enemy officials whom we employ.

"Double agents are enemy spies whom we employ.

"Expendable agents are those of our own spies who are deliberately given fabricated information to misinform the enemy."

[Chang Yu adds:

["In our dynasty, Chief of Staff Ts'ao once pardoned a condemned man, whom he then disguised as a monk and made him swallow a ball of wax and enter the enemy camp. When the false monk arrived, he was imprisoned.

["The monk told his captors about the ball of wax and soon discharged it in a stool. When the ball was opened, the enemy read a letter transmitted by Chief of Staff Ts'ao to their own Director of Strategic Planning. The chieftain of the barbarians was enraged, put his minister to death, and executed the spy monk.

["This is the idea. But expendable agents are not confined to only one use. Sometimes, I send agents to the enemy to make a covenant of peace and then I attack."]

"Living agents are those who return with information.

"Of all those in the army close to the commander, none is more intimate than the secret agent; of all rewards, none more liberal than those given to secret agents; of all matters, none is more confidential than those relating to secret operations.

"Generally, in the case of armies you wish to strike, cities you wish to attack, and people you wish to assassinate, you must know the names of the garrison commander, the staff officers, the ushers, gatekeepers, and bodyguards. You must instruct your agents to inquire into these matters in minute detail.

"Therefore, determine the enemy's plans and you will know which strategy will be successful and which will not.

"Probe him and learn where his strength is abundant and where deficient.

"Knowing the terrain is of the greatest assistance in battle. Therefore, to estimate the enemy situation and to calculate distances and the degree of difficulty of the terrain so as to control victory, are virtues of the superior general."

Negotiations:

"When the enemy's envoys speak in humble terms, but he continues his preparations, he will advance.

"When the envoys speak in apologetic terms, he wishes a respite.

"When without a previous understanding the enemy asks for a truce, he is plotting."

Tactics:

"The art of using troops is this: When ten to the enemy's one, surround him.

"If double his strength, divide him.

"If equally matched you may engage him.

"If weaker numerically, be capable of withdrawing.

"And if in all respects unequal, be capable of eluding him, for a small force is but booty for one more powerful.

"Now there are five circumstances in which victory may be predicted:

"He who knows when he can fight and when he cannot will be victorious.

"He who understands how to use both large and small forces will be victorious.

"He whose ranks are united in purpose will be victorious.

"Therefore I say: Know the enemy and know yourself; in a hundred battles you will never be in peril.

"When you are ignorant of the enemy but know yourself, your chances of winning or losing are equal.

"Generally, he who occupies the battlefield first and awaits his enemy is at ease; he who comes later to the scene and rushes into the fight is weary.

"And therefore those skilled in war bring the enemy to the field of battle and are not brought there by him.

"Appear at places to which he must hasten; move swiftly where he does not expect you.

"That you may march a thousand *li* without wearying yourself is because you travel where there is no enemy.

"When I wish to give battle, my enemy, though protected by high walls and deep moats, cannot help but engage me, for I attack a position he must defend.

"When the enemy presents an opportunity, speedily take advantage of it. Anticipate him in seizing something he values and move in accordance with a date secretly fixed.

"The doctrine of war is to follow the enemy situation in order to decide on battle.

"Therefore, at first, be shy as a maiden. When the enemy gives you an opening be swift as a hare and he will be unable to withstand you."

Surprise:

"All warfare is based on deception.

"Therefore, when capable, feign incapacity; when active, inactivity.

"When near, make it appear that you are far away; when far away, that you are near.

"Offer the enemy a bait to lure him; feign disorder and strike him.

"Where he is strong, avoid him. Attack where he is unprepared; sally out when he does not. Again, attack the mind of the opponent!

"Move when it is advantageous and create changes in the situation by dispersal and concentration of forces."

Secrecy and Speed:

"The enemy must not know where I intend to give battle. For if he does not know where I intend to give battle, he must prepare in a great many places. And when he prepares in a great many places, those I have to fight in any one place will be few.

"Speed is the essence of war. Take advantage of the enemy's unpreparedness; travel by unexpected routes and strike him where he has taken no precautions.

"The general should be capable of keeping his officers and men in ignorance of his plans.

"He changes his methods and alters his plans so that people have no knowledge of what he is doing.

"He alters his campsites and marches by devious routes, and thus makes it impossible for others to anticipate his purpose.

"Now the crux of military operations lies in the pretense of accommodating one's self to the designs of the enemy.

"Thus I say that victory can be created. For even if the enemy is numerous, I can prevent him from engaging."

Do's and Don'ts:

"Treat the captives well, and care for them.

"Do not gobble proffered baits.

"Do not attack his elite troops.

"Do not press the enemy at bay.

"When an advancing enemy crosses water, do not meet him at the water's edge. It is advantageous to allow half his force to cross and then strike.

"In war, numbers alone confer no advantage. Do not advance relying on sheer military power.

"One stays on the defense when his strength is inadequate; he attacks when it is abundant."

DOCUMENT 2

AMERICAN BACKGROUNDS: THE ROGERS' RANGERS

ABOUT THE DOCUMENT

In 1759, Major Robert Rogers, the famous American frontier soldier, laid down nineteen rules of war for his 600-man force —known as Rogers' Rangers—who won a reputation for courage and endurance in their campaign against American Indians and their French allies around Canada's Lake George. Combining silent scouting with swift surprise raids and deadly ambushes against an unsuspecting enemy, the forest-wise Rangers scored a number of successes during the Seven Years' War.

Sixty-eight years later, Rogers' Standing Orders were revived in Vietnam by General William C. Westmoreland. The U.S. commander of American soldiers stalking the Vietcong through mountains and jungle recognized that "little is really new in the art of guerrilla warfare." But the American Army had forgotten the rules of fighting that it had known at birth and that had subdued or defeated its enemies.

An experienced U.S. officer in South Vietnam said: "Today's guerrilla fighting is essentially a reversion to the old wars with the Indians. American soldiers have to go back to the old manuals and learn the simple tactics that two World Wars, in which heavy weapons played the major role, made them forget. World War I's decisive weapon was the 75-mm. howitzer; World War II was won with the armored tank and the warplane. In guerrilla warfare, the best weapon remains the light-footed, enduring infantryman and his reliable automatic rifle." The battle-wise American colonel concluded with these words: "Guerrilla fighting requires a totally different breed of foot soldier than mechanized warfare. We need tough and leathery men, patient and savvy in the knowledge of nature—soldiers who can fight in the day as in the night, in swamps as in rugged mountains. In other words, we need new Rangers."

The following are the Standing Orders of the Rogers' Rangers, in their original wording:

THE DOCUMENT

1. Don't forget nothing.
2. Have your musket clean as a whistle, hatchet scoured, sixty rounds powder and ball, and be ready to march at a minute's warning.
3. When you're on the march, act the way you would if you was sneaking up on a deer. See the enemy first.
4. Tell the truth about what you see and what you do. There is an army depending on us for correct information. You can lie all you please when you tell other folks about the rangers, but don't never lie to a ranger or officer.
5. Don't never take a chance you don't have to.
6. When we're on the march we march single file, far enough apart so one shot can't go through two men.

7. If we strike swamps, or soft ground, we spread out abreast, so it's hard to track us.

8. When we march, we keep moving till dark, so as to give the enemy the least possible chance at us.

9. When we camp, half the party stays awake while the other half sleeps.

10. If we take prisoners, we keep 'em separate till we have had time to examine them, so they can't cook up a story between 'em.

11. Don't ever march home the same way. Take a different route so you won't be ambushed.

12. No matter whether we travel in big parties or little ones, each party has to keep a scout twenty yards ahead, twenty yards on each flank and twenty yards in the rear, so the main body can't be surprised and wiped out.

13. Every night you'll be told where to meet if surrounded by a superior force.

14. Don't sit down to eat without posting sentries.

15. Don't sleep beyond dawn. Dawn's when the French and Indians attack.

16. Don't cross a river by a regular ford.

17. If somebody's trailing you, make a circle, come back onto your own tracks and ambush the folks that aim to ambush you.

18. Don't stand up when the enemy's coming against you. Kneel down, lie down, hide behind a tree.

19. Let the enemy come till he's almost close enough to touch. Then let him have it and jump out and finish him up with your hatchet.

Maj. Robert Rogers, 1759

DOCUMENT 3

GENERAL VO NGUYEN GIAP ON DIENBIENPHU

ABOUT THE DOCUMENT

So many arguments have been exchanged on Dienbienphu.
Why did the French make the mistake of going there?
Why didn't they withdraw before their enemy closed the
trap on them? Who is better prepared to answer these
questions than General Vo Nguyen Giap, the Viet Minh
commander in chief and victor of Dienbienphu, who in
one momentous battle brought an end to a century of
French military presence in Asia.

Surprisingly, General Giap—he never studied in a Western
military college, but he did have ten years of guerrilla experience behind him before attacking Dienbienphu—does
not think that French General Henri Navarre was impru-
dent in committing his best battalions in the remote North
Vietnam valley. Whatever the case, the 55-day-long Dienbienphu battle has become a classic of guerrilla warfare
as practiced by two fairly sophisticated armies: one used
conventional "bourgeois" military doctrine; the other, led
by "amateur" officers trained on the spot, improvised, as
all revolutionaries do.

Years after the battle, a North Vietnamese military commentator in Hanoi said: "If the Dienbienphu victory was undeniably a victory of the intellect, a matter of military and political leadership, one must always remember that this leadership owed its effectiveness to the extraordinary heroism of the Vietnamese people and guerrilla fighters."

Among the defeated French officers of the former Far East Expeditionary Corps, I met several who expressed similar views. Dienbienphu was one of those few historical battles about which winners and losers can be equally proud of saying "I was there." The French did not go to Dienbienphu because they underestimated their guerrilla foes; nor did they underrate General Giap's ability. All these factors had been taken into account in French military plans. What happened is that the Vietnamese, because they believed in their cause, and understood the crucial importance of the battle for their country, were prepared to achieve victory at all costs.

THE DOCUMENT

Question: Since the defeat at Dienbienphu, many French generals and politicians have been accusing General Navarre of undertaking an adventurous plan.

General Giap: When the battle is over it is easy to make accusations of all kinds against General Navarre and to assert that he should not have done this or that. While analysis is easy when the battle is over and the essential characteristics of the two opponents have been revealed, it is much more difficult to make strategic decisions when the battle is raging. To understand the Navarre Plan, we have to place it back in the context of 1953. Following the armistice in Korea, the U. S. concentrated its assistance on Indochina. The French expeditionary corps then received considerably increased aid—which was to allow it to strike decisive blows at our troops.

Thus, it was with a well-defined mission that Navarre took command in Indochina. The Navarre Plan was certainly not the least carefully studied of the operational plans drawn up by the French command in Indochina. It placed before us new and serious difficulties and, for our part, we never underestimated our adversary's capabilities.

Navarre had realized that he must at all costs carry out a large number of operations to try to regain the initiative, and he did this by concentrating forty-four mobile battalions in the Red River Delta in view of applying an appropriate strategy in the northern theatre of operations. For the French, the problem was to avert our forces' Winter-Spring offensive by carrying out powerful and swift attacks to keep our troops breathless, decimate and wear them out. And we would be forced to remain on the defensive.

The crack units of the French expeditionary force had considerable mobility; with his aircraft, motorized vehicles and ships, Navarre could move his troops from the North to the South much more easily than we could. He had been able to evacuate Na San by air, launch a raid on Langson, land troops at Tuy-hoa, airdrop others at Dienbienphu. And everybody in the Western camp was applauding, congratulating Navarre for having inspired French troops with a new dynamic spirit.

Question: How did the two armies come to face each other at Dienbienphu?

General Giap: Dienbienphu was not a part of Navarre's initial plan. When he learned that our regular divisions were moving in a north-westerly direction, he airdropped troops to occupy Dienbienphu, which, in his mind, was to

become an offensive base to paralyze our troops and prevent them from extending their operations to Laos. But the
French command was then also obsessed with another idea:
it was desperately seeking a set piece battle—which it hoped
would be decisive—with the main body of our forces. It
expected us to be crushed by French troops with all their
fire power. To our own offensive in the north-west, the
French opposed a counterplan. Dienbienphu would become
a trap into which our troops would be irresistibly lured, to
be decimated by gun fire from the formidable fortifications
of the entrenched camp.

Question: And you headed straight for the trap?

General Giap: Whether our troops or the French would
be trapped was decided by the relative strength of the
forces facing each other, and by the strategic and tactical
direction of operations. Until then we had attacked only isolated fortified positions held by relatively small French forces.
Here we had to deal with an entrenched camp with forty-
nine strong points supporting each other, and defended by
twenty-one battalions, most of which were crack French
units equipped with an impressive amount of artillery,
armor and tanks and supported by large numbers of aircraft. Our previous attacks against fortified positions, as
a rule, had lasted a single night: our troops would start
for the enemy's post at night fall, liquidate it and withdraw
before dawn. It was obvious that the battle of Dienbienphu
would last much longer. And this created new problems
for us.

Question: In order of importance, which was the first
problem?

General Giap: Logistics! The French command was not
quite wrong in thinking that the problem was for us insoluble. In previous campaigns, when we engaged in opera-

tions some hundred kilometres from our bases even with a small number of troops, we already had to content ourselves with meager soup for meal. Sometimes, we almost gave up our objective due to insufficient supply. Dienbienphu was 300 to 400 miles by road from our rear. Our forces at the front comprised several divisions. Navarre was aware of our weakness, and his air force was ceaselessly pounding our supply route. You know how we solved this problem? By the total mobilization of our people.

Question: Once supply and munitions had been secured, could you regard the problems as solved?

General Giap: They were far from solved. We still had to install our artillery on the inward slopes of the hills without having it destroyed by enemy shells. And first, how to take our guns over the hilltops surrounding Dienbienphu, when in most places there was not even a simple trail? How to approach enemy positions without being slaughtered by gun fire from his strong points and by his air force? And don't forget that our troops had to cross a fairly large plain where the adversary could use his tanks and armor. Guns had to be pulled by hand over mountain tops and hidden in cleverly camouflaged bunkers. Hundreds of miles of trenches and galleries had to be indefatigably dug during several weeks.

Question: But how did it happen that Navarre, who had an excellent intelligence network, fail to foresee all that?

General Giap: Navarre was an expert in intelligence work, and the French who ruled over our country during eighty years were pretty well acquainted with it. But Navarre, like other French generals, had made a mistake in strategy, which resulted directly from misjudgment, from total lack of knowledge of the adversary. Navarre did not realize that he was facing an entire people, a people's army waging a people's war. In fact, neither Navarre nor any other French general knew our people and our army. They largely relied on weapons, on technical means.

Question: But didn't the French command also rely on some of its crack troops?

General Giap: It did. It even indulged in paratroop-worship and Foreign Legion-worship. But it regarded these as excellent "war machines" rather than as men. Mechanical training had turned these men into robots. Fighting was their trade, but they never were told for what cause they were fighting. Relying on weaponry and mechanical training more than on the soldiers' spirit, Navarre, like all bourgeois generals, had overestimated his own strength. But a still more serious shortcoming for a general was that Navarre did not know his adversary.

Question: Many authors, especially the military men, have blamed Navarre for this. They have given the impression that another general would not have made Navarre's Dienbienphu error. What do you think of this opinion?

General Giap: As I told you, it is easy to give judgment on what has happened. If those "experts" had had to command the French Expeditionary Corps in 1953-1954, perhaps they would not have sought a strategic decision at Dienbienphu, but in any case they would have committed their troops elsewhere, and any plan of theirs would have been foiled by us. Those who freely used tanks, planes and artillery could hardly understand how such poorly armed combatants could oppose them.

DOCUMENT 4

CHE GUEVARA ON GUERRILLA WARFARE

ABOUT THE DOCUMENT

From 1956, when he was one of the few survivors of a
Castro-led rebel landing in Cuba, to 1959, when he commanded the rebel troops that occupied Havana's famous La
Cabana fortress, Major Ernesto "Che" Guevara fought as
one of the top leaders in the Cuban Revolution. After the
rebel victory Major Guevara wrote his book *Guerrilla Warfare* to synthesize the experiences of that struggle. It has
become the authoritative handbook for guerrilla and counter
guerrilla activities on the American continent. In 1968, Major
Guevara was assassinated in Bolivia after his capture by
American-trained troops. The following is the introductory
chapter of *Guerrilla Warfare,* in which Major Guevara defined the essence of guerrilla strategy:

THE DOCUMENT

We consider that the Cuban Revolution contributed three
fundamental lessons to the conduct of revolutionary movements in America. They are:

236 AGE OF THE GUERRILLA

1. Popular forces can win a war against the army.
2. It is not necessary to wait until all conditions making revolution exist; the insurrection can create them.
3. In underdeveloped America the countryside is the basic area for armed fighting. . .

Guerrilla warfare, the basis of the struggle of a people to redeem itself, has diverse characteristics, different facets, even though the essential will for liberation remains the same. It is obvious—and writers on the theme have said it many times—that war responds to a certain series of scientific laws; whoever ignores them will go down to defeat . . .

Our task at the moment is to find the basic principles of this kind of fighting and the rules to be followed by peoples seeking liberation; to develop theory from facts; to generalize and give structure to our experience for the profit of others.

Let us first consider the question: who are the combatants in guerrilla warfare? On one side we have a group composed of the oppressor and his agents—the professional army, well armed and disciplined, in many cases receiving foreign help as well as the help of the bureaucracy in the employ of the oppressor. On the other side are the people of the nation or region involved. It is important to emphasize that guerrilla warfare is a war of the masses, a war of the people. The guerrilla band is an armed nucleus, the fighting vanguard of the people. . . [It] is used by the side that is supported by a majority but that possesses a much smaller number of arms for use in defense against oppression. . . . We must come to the inevitable conclusion that the guerrilla fighter is a social reformer, that he takes up arms responding to the angry protest of the people against their oppressors, and that he fights in order to change the social system that keeps all his unarmed brothers in ignominy and misery. He launches himself against the conditions of the reigning institutions at a particular moment and dedicates himself with all the vigor that circumstances permit to breaking the mold of those institutions.

When we analyze more fully the tactic of guerrilla warfare, we will see that the guerrilla fighter needs to have a good knowledge of the surrounding countryside, the paths of entry and escape, the possibilities of speedy maneuver, good hiding places; naturally, also, he must count on the support of the people. All this indicates that the guerrilla fighter will carry out his action in wild places of small population. Since in these places the struggle of the people for reforms is aimed primarily and also exclusively at changing the social form of land ownership, the guerrilla fighter is above all an agrarian revolutionary. . . .

There is a malevolent definition that says: "The guerrilla fighter is the Jesuit of warfare." By this is indicated a quality of secretiveness, of treachery, of surprise that is obviously an essential element of guerrilla warfare. It is a special kind of Jesuitism, naturally prompted by circumstances, which necessitates acting at certain moments in ways different from the romantic and sporting conceptions with which we are taught to believe war is fought.

War is always a struggle in which each contender tries to annihilate the other. Besides using force, they will have recourse to all possible tricks and stratagems in order to achieve the goal. Military strategy and tactics are a representation by analysis of the objectives of groups and of the means of achieving these objectives. These means contemplate taking advantage of all the weak points of the enemy.

. . . It is always possible to carry out guerrilla attacks in such a way as to assure surprise; and it is the duty of the guerrilla fighter to do so.

"Hit and run," some call this scornfully, and this is accurate. Hit and run, wait, lie in ambush, again hit and run, and thus repeatedly, without giving any rest to the enemy. There is in all this, it would appear, a negative quality, an attitude of retreat, of avoiding frontal fights. However, this is consequent upon the general strategy of guerrilla warfare, which is the same in its ultimate end as is any warfare: to win, to annihilate the enemy.

Thus it is clear that guerrilla warfare is a phase that does not afford in itself opportunities to arrive at complete victory. It is one of the initial phases of warfare and will develop continuously until the guerrilla army in its steady growth acquires the characteristics of a regular army. At that moment it will be ready to deal final blows to the enemy and to achieve victory. Triumph will always be the product of a regular army, even though its origins are in a guerrilla army.

Just as the general of a division in a modern war does not have to die in front of his soldiers, the guerrilla fighter, who is general of himself, need not die in every battle. He is ready to give his life, but the positive quality of this guerrilla warfare is precisely that each one of the guerrilla fighters is ready to die, not to defend an ideal, but rather to convert it into reality. This is the basis, the essence, of guerrilla fighting. Miraculously, a small band of men, the armed vanguard of the great popular force that supports them, goes beyond the immediate tactical objective, goes on decisively to achieve an ideal, to establish a new society, to break the old molds of the outdated, and to achieve, finally, the social justice for which they fight.

DOCUMENT 5

FIDEL CASTRO'S SECOND DECLARATION AT HAVANA

ABOUT THE DOCUMENT

The following is the speech made by Fidel Castro at an open-air assembly of more than a million people at the Plaza of the Revolution, Havana, February 4, 1962. It is the political sequel to the First Declaration of Havana, in which the immediate practical goals of the Cuban Revolution were set forth. In the Second Declaration Fidel Castro, in the name of his government—expressed the appeal of guerrilla revolutions for Latin Americans. The premise is simple—thousands of Latin Americans are dying because of the backward social conditions of their countries; they would risk little more in a struggle for change. Castro only implied the alternative course in the document that follows, but he stated it explicitly in later speeches.

THE DOCUMENT

. . . We cannot forget the picture of weak, uncared-for children, Latin America's children without a future. Latin

America is a continent with a high birth rate. It is also a
continent with a high death rate. Just a few years ago, the
death rate for children in their first year of life, in eleven
countries, was as high as 125 per thousand; in seventeen
more countries, 90 per thousand. At the same time, in 102
countries throughout the world, this figure is 51 per thousand. In Latin America 74 additional children die in their
first year of life for lack of care. There are countries in
Latin America where this percentage reaches 300 per thousand.

Thousands and thousands of children under the age of
seven die due to shocking causes: diarrhea, pneumonia, mal-
nutrition, famine. Thousands and thousands die without
hospital attention, without medicine. Thousands and thousands more walk about with ailments such as endemic cre-
tinism, malaria, tracoma, and other infermities produced by
contamination, by lack of clean water and other necessities.
. . . Summing up this nightmare in which Latin America
lives, from one end to the other, it must be said that in this
continent of almost 200 million human beings—two thirds
of whom are Indians, mestizos and Negroes—four persons
a minute die of premature old age or of diseases that are
curable. A total of 5,500 die every day, two million every
year, ten million every five years. These deaths can be
avoided easily, but they happen just the same. Two thirds of
the Latin American population live little and that little is
under the constant threat of death. It is a holocaust that in
fifteen years has caused more deaths than the First World
War, and it continues.

Meanwhile, from Latin America to the United States
streams a continuous flow of money: $4,000 every minute,
$5,000,000 every day, two billion dollars every year, ten bil-
lion dollars every five years. For each thousand dollars that

we lose, we receive a corpse. A thousand dollars per corpse. This is the price of what is called imperialism. A THOUSAND DOLLARS A CORPSE, FOUR TIMES A MINUTE! . . . .

From the dawn of independence the poor man's destiny has been the same. Indians, gauchos, mestizos, zambos, mulatos, whites without land or income—all this human mass that stood in the ranks of a nation that was never theirs, those who fell by the millions, that were edged out, that won independence from Europe for the business men, who were thrown out of the cities, and who continue to occupy the bottom rung of social benefits—continue to die of hunger, of curable diseases, of lack of attention, because they were never able to attain the saving graces: bread, a bed in a hospital, good medicine, a helping hand.

But now is the hour of their vindication. The hour they have selected. They are calling forth, now, from one end of the continent to the other. Now this anonymous mass, this colored America—sombre, taciturn—that sings throughout the whole continent with the same sadness and despair, now it is this mass that begins to enter into its own, historically, that begins to write history with its blood, that begins to suffer and die for this. Because now, in the fields and mountains of Latin America, on the slopes of its *sierras,* on its plains and in its jungles, in solitude or amidst the traffic of cities, on the coasts of great oceans and rivers, this world begins to shake with new logic. It shakes with the fists of those who would die for what is theirs, to win by conquest the rights that have been denied them for over five hundred years by various establishments. Now, yes, history will have to count the poor of Latin America. . . .

APPENDIX

APPENDIX: 1

WHAT MOTIVATES
THE GUERRILLA?

Why does the guerrilla fight? If he is a soldier infiltrated behind enemy lines, his motivation is patriotism or a taste for adventure and thrills. If he is a social reformer, like Castro, he takes up arms in response to a protest movement, or creates it. But there are many other causes and reasons why guerrilla movements are born, from the hunger for land of an Indian peasant to the ingrained irredentism of an Arab nationalist. Herewith is a list of the most frequent types of motivation observed among guerrillas, with some of the countries where they played a dominant role.

a) Resistance against a foreign presence (Europe during the German occupation).
b) Freedom wars (Algeria, South Yemen).
c) Racial survival (the Kurds of Iraq, Biafra, etc.).
d) Social revolutions (China, Cuba, etc.).
e) Religious rights (the Somalis in Kenya and Ethiopia, the Tibetans in China).

f) Anti-establishment (the Pathet Lao in Laos, the Free Khmer movement in Cambodia, the Thai Patriotic Front in Thailand).

g) Anti-imperialism (Indonesia's "confrontation" with Malaysia).

h) Neutralism (in Vietnam, the installation of a neutralist regime is publicized as the "immediate" or "tactical" cause, while "class struggle" would be the long-range or "strategic" cause).

i) Land hunger: (the peasant revolts of India).

j) Economic objectives (the opium war in Laos).

k) Wars of liberation influenced by Marxist ideology (Several guerrilla movements in Latin America and in Southeast Asia).

APPENDIX: 2

THE MANY DIFFERENT TYPES OF GUERRILLA WAR

Trying to categorize the guerrilla wars taking place since the end of World War II can be a very confusing undertaking. Many guerrilla wars, which initially started with one popular cause, such as independence or political freedom, have become sidetracked by their leaders toward more permanent objectives: social revolution or the dictatorship of a party, of a clan, or of an ideology. Below is a list of the categories of guerrilla wars, most of which have been encountered in this volume. Some overlapping is occasionally unavoidable. To name only one example, the Vietnam war started as an anticolonial movement to bring freedom and independence to a nation. Later it became an ideological conflict and a social revolution.

1. *The residual conflicts of World War II* (1945-1949)

Greece	Indonesia
Iran (The Tudeh insurrection)	Malaya
	The Philippines
Indochina	China's civil war

2. *The Cold War conflicts* (1949-1954)

Greece again
Korea
Indochina (after 1950)

3. *The anticolonial movements*

Algeria	Cyprus
Tunisia	Southeast Asia

4. *Troublesome nationalists*

Palestine's Arabs and Jews	Indonesia vs. West New Guinea
Indonesia's confrontation with Malaysia	Aden, the South Arabian Federation and FLOSY
Egypt in Yemen	The Kashmir dispute

5. *Social revolution in Latin America*

Guatemala	Cuba
Dominican Republic	Venezuela
Bolivia	Colombia
Peru	

APPENDIX: 3

THE PHASES OF GUERRILLA WARFARE

The organizational work for a guerrilla movement begins with care. This is the inception phase, when the leaders seek out persons loyal to the cause for use as contacts, carriers of weapons, and guides. Then comes the buildup of the guerrilla army, where tactics have to be invented to break up the reaction of and encirclement by the enemy. Gradually, the guerrillas achieve an equilibrium of power with their adversary, or they fail and then face annihilation. Some strategists call this "the second phase" of guerrilla warfare. The third phase comes when the balance of power is in favor of the guerrilla. The important thing then is to inflict the *coup de grace* to the enemy and realize the political objectives of the movement. But between inception and realization, the long road to success is fragmented into many intermediate steps. Some of these steps follow:

1: Strategic planning. This phase requires utmost secrecy.

2: Setting in place the clandestine political infrastructure of the movement: recruiting of couriers, messengers, etc.

3: Psychological operations to dramatize the cause of the guerrillas at home and abroad. As much publicity as possible is to be given to the political platform of the movement.

4: Selective terrorism to eliminate potential opponents of the insurgency in the countryside.

5: Sabotage of lines of communication to isolate the territorial base areas of the guerrilla.

6: Creation of safe areas and strongholds to shelter command headquarters—usually in sparse mountainous regions.

7: Development of liberated areas in populated rural regions to be administered by the guerrillas.

8: Proselytization among the enemy to entice defectors and ruin his morale.

9: Gradual strangulation of cities by the rural areas under guerrilla control. Organization of the urban population for civil disobedience.

10: A general offensive carried out by a liberation army to knock out the last vestiges of government presence.

11: Negotiations to formalize the transfer of power to the political forces born from the guerrilla movement.

APPENDIX: 4

PACIFICATION DEFINED

Pacification is the use of military and civilian personnel to
restore law and order and the basic functions of government
—education, administration, public health, etc.—in a region
recently freed from guerrilla control. One important aspect
of pacification is the uprooting of "dormant" political agents
and secret cells left behind by guerrilla fighters. The task
requires close cooperation between civilian police forces, administration personnel, and the military units assigned to
pacification.

Unless a civilian population is persuaded to cooperate actively with the troops, the task of pacification is—in most
cases—a long, arduous, frustrating process. Several years
after the end of the Malayan insurgency, Malay troops and
police forces were still absorbed in the pacification of remote rural areas near the Thai border, where the political
influence of Chinese guerrillas, defeated many years before,
was still being felt.

INDEX